Birth Of A City

Carl Morgan

COVER PHOTO: Ouellette Avenue looking north.
See details on Page 87.

Canadian Cataloguing in Publication Data

Morgan, Carl
        Birth of a city

ISBN 1-895305-02-0 (bound) - ISBN 1-895305-03-9 (pbk.)

1. Windsor (Ont.) — History.   I. Title.

FC3099.W56M67 1991   971.3'32   C91-090425-1
F1059.5.W5M67 1991

TraveLife
12402 Riverside Drive East
Tecumseh, Ontario, Canada
N8N 1A3

Typesetting & Design: Benchmark Publishing & Design
                          1275 Walker Road
                          Windsor, Ontario, Canada
                          N8Y 4X9

Printed by Border Press Inc., Windsor.

Contents

This book is dedicated to the determined men and women whose tireless efforts throughout the years have helped to fashion Windsor into the remarkable City it is today.

Acknowledgements

In the early days of 1990 (a lifetime ago) when I began sketching an outline for this book, I had only a few, faint ideas about the story I thought I wanted to tell. I wasn't entirely sure whether it would work, and I certainly didn't know how I would get to wherever it was I was going.

Having published another book several years before, I was still painfully mindful of the enormous amount of pure, heavy slogging that I would face, and I braced myself for what I expected to be a long, lonely Odyssey.

Thankfully, I was half wrong. It was long – but not lonely. By the time I reached the mid-way point, so many people were assisting or offering encouragement that I realized it had evolved into somewhat of a community project.

Now it is time to extend my warmest words of appreciation to the many people who "were there" when needed: those who made important suggestions, guided me with constructive criticism, pointed me in challenging directions, lent me material from treasured collections, gave freely of their time to read the manuscript, or simply said, "good luck".

Before even the first word was written, I was offered full resource support by Windsor Star Publisher Jim Thomson. That support was quantified over many months by the entire photo department under the direction of Photo Editor Bill Bishop and Photo Supervisor (now retired) Stan Andrews; full research support was also given by The Star's library staff under Deborah Jessop, Head of the paper's Library Information Services. Without her persistent interest and effort, there would have been many embarrassing flaws in the fabric of the story.

Unequivocal words of thanks are extended to a number of institutions and staff members for their invaluable contributions:

Hiram Walker, Allied Vintners.

Hiram Walker Historical Museum; Alan Douglas, Curator Emeritus; Susan Hughes, now Curator Todmorden Museum, Toronto.

Hotel Dieu Hospital; Sister Aurore Beaulieu, Superior of the Religious Hospitallers of St. Joseph in Windsor.

Municipal Archives—Windsor Public Library; Mark Walsh, Archivist and Linda Chakmak, Assistant Archivist.

North American Black Historical Museum; Betty Simpson, Director; Barbara Habib, former Administrator.

St. John's Anglican Church, Sandwich; Rev. Christopher Pratt, Pastor.

Sisters of the Holy Names of Jesus and Mary

University of Windsor, Leddy Library; Bill Jackson, Reader Services Librarian; Conrad Reitz, Librarian.

Windsor Public Library; Erika Rebello, Assistant Specialist, Literature and History.

Fort Malden National Historic Sites; Harry Bosveld, Superintendent.

Words of sincere appreciation are also due to private collectors, Howard Watts, Margaret Westgate and Don Wilson, who generously lent me material from their unique collections; to Larry Kulisek, Associate Professor of History, University of Windsor, who shared his deep knowledge of this area's history to help clarify conflicting information.

I am especially grateful to those who readily agreed to the thankless task of reading the raw manuscript and proofs before publication. These include Evelyn McLean, Heritage Planner, Planning Department, City of Windsor; Michael Power, Historian; Al Roach, retired Teacher and Author; Ronald Hoskins, Associate Professor of History, University of Windsor; Linda Chakmak, Alan Douglas, Susan Hughes, Deborah Jessop and Mark Walsh.

I am particularly indebted to the Essex County Historical Association and the City of Windsor's Architectural Conservation Advisory Committee (WACAC) for allowing me to draw valuable material unreservedly from their many important publications. Without such access, it would have been impossible to complete Birth Of A City in the form that it is.

Photo credits that read "CITY OF WINDSOR (WACAC)" refer to material made available through the City's Architectural Conservation Advisory Committee.

While the final responsibility for everything that appears between these covers is mine, the vital role that these friends played cannot be overstated. Without their attention to detail there would have been many unfortunate gaffes.

Credit for the creative design is due to the manifold skills of Karen Monck, Mary MacKay and Veryle Monck of Windsor's Benchmark Publishing & Design.

Finally, a word of apology and deep appreciation to my wife, Gloria, who endured many lonely hours as I tapped out the hundreds of thousands of words which were finally distilled to the comparatively few that comprise this book. Throughout it all she encouraged me constantly, but chided as well, saying that in the final months, the book had become as obsessively demanding as a live-in mistress.

Now, it is done, with thanks to all.

Foreword

By the time the 1992 Centennial Celebration Committee was set up by Windsor City Council in the spring of 1990, *Birth Of A City* had already been on Carl Morgan's mental drawing board for some time. Although the finished product bears the Centennial logo, it was Carl's idea and his idea alone which grew into the book presently before the reader.

It has been a pleasure for me to have watched the development of this book from three vantage points — first in my capacity as an archivist; second, as one among many in Windsor's community of heritage professionals reading the book before publication, at Carl's invitation; and third, as a member of the 1992 Centennial Celebration Committee, encouraging Carl to have his book associated with the 100th anniversary of Windsor's incorporation as a city. From all three vantages, one perspective comes forward. *Birth Of A City* stands out as a remarkable book.

In the pages which follow, Carl Morgan tells the reader that "sometimes history, like beauty, is in the eye of the beholder." That being the case, we are all indebted to Carl for his vision of Windsor's past. The book is written from a popular history approach which reaches the reader in the unique and immediate manner to which all good historical writings aspire, but too few achieve. It draws us back into Windsor's past with a deep sense of familiarity about the events and personalities described. The author as the beholder of Windsor's history has succeeded in weaving the strands of this community's heritage into a warm and colourful fabric, which clothes us all.

"Come celebrate with us" is the motto of the 1992 Centennial Celebration. *Birth Of A City* clearly shows one of Windsor's most precious resources truly worth celebrating — our history. The book is in itself a celebration of this resource. Enjoy.

G. Mark Walsh
1992 Centennial Celebration Committee.

Footnotes:

Throughout the pages of *Birth Of A City*, there are many references to the Hiram Walker Historical Museum. As the final proofreading was being carried out in preparation for publication, consideration was being given to changing the name of the museum to: *François Baby House (Windsor's Community Museum)*.

There are several mentions of buildings being located, or events having taken place, on Sandwich Street in Windsor. Although Sandwich Street did originally connect Windsor with the old town of Sandwich, the Windsor stretch of Sandwich Street was renamed and is now known as Riverside Drive.

Introduction

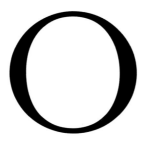One hundred years ago, on Tuesday, May 24, 1892, Queen Victoria's birthday, Windsor, ever the scrappy, pugnacious bordertown brat from the wrong side of the river, shed the trappings of adolescence and proudly donned the mantle of cityhood.

The years leading up to that historic event were filled with excitement, challenge and adventure; they were the most fascinating and intriguing of this area's long, historic and colourful past.

Unfortunately the passage of time has not been kind to our collective consciousness, so that today those heritage years are among the least known or understood by generations of descendants and newcomers alike.

During those troublesome, growing-up times, this community, which started life as an unremarkable, muddy little river town, a stepchild without even a name of its own, finally completed its metamorphosis and emerged, strutting and flexing its muscles as one of this young country's proud, brash and even younger upstarts.

Census records tell us that the city's population climbed from 200 in 1836 when it was named *Windsor*, to 750 in 1854 when it received its charter as a village.

By 1892 the population had reached 10,500 — and growing.

On the 24th of May that year they held a party for this cocky new kid on the block and he strutted and preened for all to see as soldiers marched, bands played, flags waved and voices cheered until they were hoarse.

It was a day to remember.

Now, as we acknowledge our age and our maturity and celebrate our 100th Birthday, it is the right moment to reflect on our all-but-forgotten past . . . to

Sandwich Street looking east from Ouellette Avenue.

fill the gaps in our understanding ... to recall the people who came and settled here, particularly those who laid the foundation stones for the city we know today.

It is to the memory of those people that this book is dedicated.

Why they came and how they got here would fill another book — but they did — those restless, God-fearing men and women of the 18th and 19th Centuries. It surely took a massive injection of desperation, of ingenuity and of sheer stubborness — perhaps even bordering on madness, to carve a shallow toe-hold . . . to simply survive in an unmapped land as unforgiving to the careless or the weak as any place on earth.

Because they did, because they survived, it is now etched into the history books of our country, that the cradle settlement of Ontario is the historic Western District which embraces the Detroit River Border Region.

Within this Western District, the first permanent European settlement was being established while the rest of the province was still an uncharted wilderness.

It was here, on the far western edge of that Western District that Windsor — and Ontario — were born.

Ironically, with the exception of a handful of dedicated history buffs, few people fully understand that Windsor, as a cornerstone of the Border Region, remains today one of the most historically important communities in Ontario.

Alan Douglas, Curator Emeritus of the Hiram Walker Historical Museum, (which stands on a parcel of land that was a pivotal staging point in the Battle of 1812) has noted, with justifiable pride, that this area boasts more history per square inch than any other region in the province.

Sadly, circumstances have not been on our side, and today, only a few signposts remain to guide those who choose to trace the early steps of the French pioneers, the missionaries, the explorers and the first settlers.

It wasn't always that way; there have been fine homes and hotels and ferry landings and academies of learning which, if they existed today, would present an exciting mosaic of what the

Barracks Square, now City Hall Square, was the community's "common", a popular gathering place in the 19th Century. St. Alphonsus Church and St. Mary's Academy are visible in the background.

community once was. Fire, recessions, depressions, human carelessness, thoughtlessness, shortsightedness and a host of events, natural and otherwise, have all played a part in erasing too many traces of the past. As custodians of our heritage, we have not carried our responsibilities well.

Birth Of A City is a combined anecdotal notebook and photo album focussing on selected events from our past. It takes us from the earliest days through to 1892 — the year that Windsor, The City, was born.

It does not pretend to be a definitive history of the Western District. Other books by other authors have already done that well enough.

The story of Windsor is not the story of a single community; it is the story of three communities — Windsor, Sandwich and Walkerville — the original Border Cities. While they remained separate kissing-cousins until 1935, their historical and geographical associations have been so tightly woven through the years that it would make no sense to talk about one without the others.

Finally, the story of Windsor is more than a textbook recitation of dates and places and times. The real story is of the people who walked its river banks, its meadows and its streets; people like Sir Isaac Brock; Tecumseh, the Shawnee Indian Chief; Henry Bibb, publisher of the first black newspaper in Sandwich; Alexander Mackenzie, Canada's second prime minister; Mary Ann Shadd, a remarkable, single-minded black activist who became Canada's first female editor/publisher; Hiram Walker, distiller, grain merchant, businessman, entrepreneur; Oscar Fleming, first mayor of the City of Windsor.

That is what this book is really about.

Some critics will argue that certain events have received less attention than deserved, while others received too much. There is no easy response except to offer a sincere word of apology for any inadvertent indiscretions and add that sometimes history, like beauty, is in the eye of the beholder.

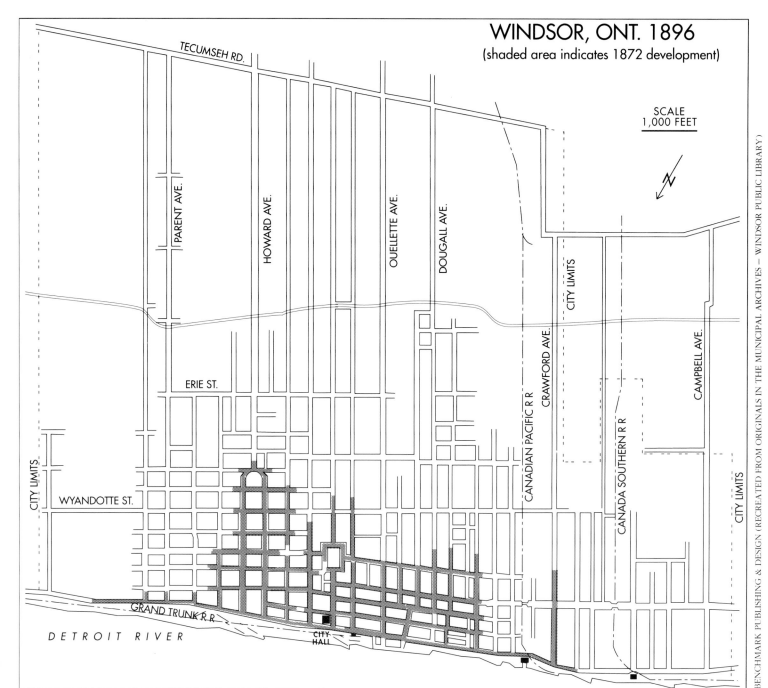

WINDSOR, ONT. 1896
(shaded area indicates 1872 development)

SCALE
1,000 FEET

TECUMSEH RD.

PARENT AVE.

HOWARD AVE.

OUELLETTE AVE.

DOUGALL AVE.

CANADIAN PACIFIC R R

CRAWFORD AVE.

CITY LIMITS

CANADA SOUTHERN R R

CAMPBELL AVE.

CITY LIMITS

ERIE ST.

CITY LIMITS

WYANDOTTE ST.

GRAND TRUNK R R

CITY HALL

DETROIT RIVER

Although no maps are known to exist showing Windsor boundaries in 1892, this recreated composite shows the growth that took place between 1872, twenty years before inauguration (shaded area), and the much expanded community of 1896, four years after inauguration.

BENCHMARK PUBLISHING & DESIGN (RECREATED FROM ORIGINALS IN THE MUNICIPAL ARCHIVES – WINDSOR PUBLIC LIBRARY)

Part One:

The Romance Of Windsor

1892: The Way We Were

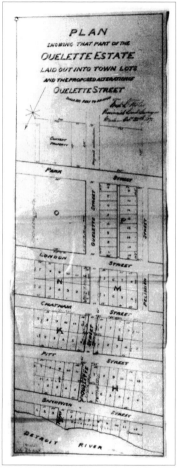

1871 street map shows the proposed "Ouellette Estate" and the extension of Ouellette Avenue south of Park Street.

I t was a good time to be growing up in Canada; to be growing up in Windsor — a proud and feisty place that elbowed its way up from a muddy little stagecoach hamlet in 1828 ... to a village in 1854 ... to a robust frontier town in 1858 and now, as a fledgling city, would soon blossom into the mercantile and political heart of the Western District of Upper Canada.

It was 1892, the spring of the year, traditionally a time of renewal; there was a good feeling, a freshness in the air; there was a sense of spunkiness, a sense of progress, a sense of knowing who you were and where you were going.

Mayor Oscar E. Fleming had spearheaded Windsor's drive for city status in 1891. Now, little more than a year later, his mission complete and having been elected as the first mayor of the *CITY* of Windsor, he watched with satisfaction as preparations were made to celebrate Windsor's debut.

It was a good time to be taking your place as one of the newest cities in a land which itself was a fresh and bright and shiny as a new-mint copper penny ... a country so young that it, too was only then preparing to celebrate its first quarter-century of nationhood.

As is so often the case, a chance word, a flip of the coin, a roll of the dice will determine the destiny of a single individual, a family — or a city. In this instance, the decision to establish the western terminus of the Great Western Railway in Windsor instead of Amherstburg or Sandwich, as had been pondered earlier, tipped the scales and confirmed the city's logistical importance as the transportation centre of the Western District.

When the GWR introduced regular rail service in January 1854, it opened a new world of opportunity for those who came: their thin, worn carpet bags packed with meagre personal belongings, their hearts bursting with dreams of

Two flourishing hotels during the mid-1800s were the Hirons House (right) and its successor, the British American (below). Hirons was in existence first. After the fire of 1871, the "BA" was built, virtually as an extension of Hirons on the same site at the northeast corner of Ouellette Avenue and Riverside Drive. The British American was demolished in 1975 and part of the foundation was preserved, now forming part of the Dieppe Gardens landscape near the Udine fountain.

happier, more fulfilling lives taming the undeveloped frontier.

This wave of immigration brought hundreds of families from cities, towns and farms in the East. Most would press on, crossing the border to find their destinies in the Midwest; others paused long enough to see fresh opportunities on this side of the border, to stay and put down roots.

A second major surge occurred in 1890 when the Canadian Pacific Railway arrived to challenge its chief rival, the Grand Trunk which had by then absorbed Great Western. It was Sir William Van Horne, president of the CPR, and astute businessman who, realizing that productive salt mines existed in Michigan, had a hunch that the deposits probably extended to the Canadian side as well.

Tests on the CPR right-of-way in Windsor proved him right; a plant was erected on the railway's Sandwich Street property near Crawford. Overnight, the CPR — and Windsor — were in the salt mining business.

Birth Of A City

One of the first commercial electric streetcars in North America was built in Windsor and made its debut with a run between Windsor and Walkerville on May 24, 1886.

Although Windsor's years leading to the final decade of the 19th Century had been uncertain, this spring season there was an unusual sense of confidence in the air; not only could you feel it, but if you looked around, you could see it.

Those who rode the electric street car, or strolled along the newly-paved streets, or stood in the glow of the new electric lights, knew it.

Certainly the 205 customers of Alexander Graham Bell's revolutionary telephone system knew it.

It's interesting to note, though, that the idea of moving from town to city status was not universally applauded.

On Friday, January 8, 1892, the Windsor *Weekly Record* reported:

> *"The following is the vote polled on Monday for incorporation:*
> *For 701: Against 502."*

(Sources: 49, 54)

The Windsor Post Office opened in 1880 at what is now Pitt Street and Ouellette Avenue.

Fleming: Last Mayor Of The Town, First Mayor Of The City

If ever one person earned a page in local history books as a hard-driving Canadian dreamer and doer — a man with a mission — it would be O.E. Fleming, the man who has the distinction of being the last mayor of the Town of Windsor in 1891 and the first mayor of the City of Windsor in 1892.

It was Fleming who, during his first term as mayor of the town in 1891, led the successful campaign to have Windsor incorporated as a city the following year.

Fleming, who was born in Milton but raised in Windsor, was admitted to the bar when he was 24. In time he was recognized as one of Ontario's prominent lawyers.

After graduation, he returned to Windsor and became involved in city politics. He first won a school board seat, serving as a trustee from 1887 through 1889. He then won a council seat in 1890 which led to his election as mayor the following year at the age of 30.

Once in office, he lost no time focussing on what he judged to be the serious business of the day — becoming a city. That message was part of his inaugural address on January 18, 1891 in which he warned that in the year ahead, council would have to deal with at least seven matters of special importance. They included the town water supply ... a $50,000 local improvement programme ... introduction of a board of health, and:

" ... *city incorporation, which matter should be fully investigated. A public meeting of citizens out to be promoted and the council guided largely by the sentiment of such meeting ... "*

In later years Fleming was instrumental in the formation of the Essex Border Utilities Commission and was involved with the building of Metropolitan General Hospital.

He was a friend of Sir Adam Beck, who had earned a reputation as a hard-driving businessman, a manufacturer, dynamic politician and the principal founding father of Ontario Hydro Electric Power Commission. Fleming and Beck worked aggressively for the establishment of Ontario Hydro as well as the Canadian Deep

Mayor Oscar E. Fleming led the battle for Windsor to seek status as a city. He was the last mayor of the Town of Windsor and the first mayor of the City of Windsor.

CITY OF WINDSOR

Waterways and Power Association. He became the association's first president, leading a successful international drive to deepen the St. Lawrence waterways, which allowed ocean ships to reach Great Lakes ports including Windsor and Walkerville.

That important effort was recognized and posthumously in 1958 when a portion of the Detroit River was named the Fleming Channel in his honour and a granite memorial was erected at Windsor's Alexander Park on the shores of the Detroit River.

(Sources: 49, 54)

Hear Ye!

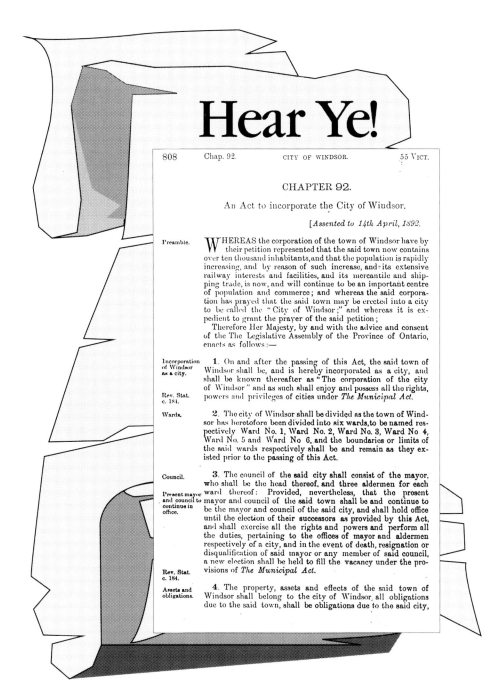

CHAPTER 92.

An Act to incorporate the City of Windsor.

[*Assented to 14th April, 1892.*]

Preamble. WHEREAS the corporation of the town of Windsor have by their petition represented that the said town now contains over ten thousand inhabitants, and that the population is rapidly increasing, and by reason of such increase, and its extensive railway interests and facilities, and its mercantile and shipping trade, is now, and will continue to be an important centre of population and commerce; and whereas the said corporation has prayed that the said town may be erected into a city to be called the "City of Windsor;" and whereas it is expedient to grant the prayer of the said petition;

Therefore Her Majesty, by and with the advice and consent of the The Legislative Assembly of the Province of Ontario, enacts as follows :—

Incorporation of Windsor as a city. 1. On and after the passing of this Act, the said town of Windsor shall be, and is hereby incorporated as a city, and shall be known thereafter as "The corporation of the city of Windsor" and as such shall enjoy and possess all the rights, **Rev. Stat. c. 184.** powers and privileges of cities under *The Municipal Act.*

Wards. 2. The city of Windsor shall be divided as the town of Windsor has heretofore been divided into six wards, to be named respectively Ward No. 1, Ward No. 2, Ward No. 3, Ward No 4, Ward No. 5 and Ward No 6, and the boundaries or limits of the said wards respectively shall be and remain as they existed prior to the passing of this Act.

Council. 3. The council of the said city shall consist of the mayor, who shall be the head thereof, and three aldermen for each **Present mayor and council to continue in office.** ward thereof: Provided, nevertheless, that the present mayor and council of the said town shall be and continue to be the mayor and council of the said city, and shall hold office until the election of their successors as provided by this Act, and shall exercise all the rights and powers and perform all the duties, pertaining to the offices of mayor and aldermen respectively of a city, and in the event of death, resignation or disqualification of said mayor or any member of said council, a new election shall be held to fill the vacancy under the pro- **Rev. Stat. c. 184.** visions of *The Municipal Act.*

Assets and obligations. 4. The property, assets and effects of the said town of Windsor shall belong to the city of Windsor, all obligations due to the said town, shall be obligations due to the said city,

Let the Record Show ...

Once the notion was accepted that Windsor should seek city status, action by civic officials was swift. Following are excerpts from some of the minutes, letters and notices culled from the files of the Municipal Archives—Windsor Public Library.

January 19, 1891, A Council Resolution:
Moved by Mr. Sutherland ... that the Mayor be requested to call a public meeting of ratepayers for Tuesday evening, the 27th instant, to discuss the question of the erection of the Town of Windsor into a City ...

NOTICE OF PUBLIC MEETING
ON CITY INCORPORATION

A public meeting of the ratepayers will be held at the Music Hall on Tuesday, January 27, 1891 at 7:30 o'clock p.m. for the purpose of discussing the question of the erection of the Town of Windsor into a City
By request of the Council
O.E. Fleming, Mayor
Windsor, January 21, 1891

Extract from Mayor Fleming's Inaugural Address, Jan. 18, 1892
"... City incorporation was a matter in respect to which the Council will be required to act. Notice of application for a special Act has been given, the popular vote was in favour of the change...

Letter from City Clerk to Police Commission, April 19, 1892
I am instructed by the Council to notify you that an Act has been passed by the Legislature of Ontario, erecting the Town of Windsor into a city 'to enjoy and possess all the rights, powers and privileges under the Municipal Act ...'

On May 24, 1892, A New City Is Born

It was one of those picture-perfect spring days: A light, caressing breeze played tease-tag with cottonball clouds, bobbing and skipping in unfettered delight across a sky, clear and blue as the finest Wedgwood.

It was the kind of day that made heavy hearts light and forced lingering memories of bitter winter months to retreat like the last traces of a morning fog.

If you could pick any day you wanted as the day to celebrate your city's first birthday, the best would be this one — Tuesday, May 24, 1892.

Making it doubly important, it was also the day the British Empire celebrated the 73rd birthday of Queen Victoria. She was also marking her 55th year as monarch.

The city had come awake early this Tuesday morning and even now the clock on the tower overlooking the low-slung wooden army barracks in City Square, showed that it was not yet nine o'clock. There was still more than an hour to wait before the big event — the Trades and Society Procession — would begin.

People were in a party mood; streets were alive with the sights and sounds of excited celebrants; mongrel dogs added to the bedlam, running among skittish horses, yapping at the heels of little boys with hoops, doing tricks for little girls who were cuddling rag dolls and pretending not to notice.

The ladies, prim in their cotton prints, scolded their men for tardiness; the men grumbled, running thick fingers inside the stiff rim of starched collars; toes were already raw from the chafing of heavy black boots normally endured only at weddings, funerals and sabbath services.

From the distance came the spirited strains of patriotic marching music as the 21st Fusiliers and the Toronto Grenadiers, one of the country's leading military bands, tuned their instruments for the parade.

The Grenadiers had left Toronto by train at ten o'clock Saturday night and arrived in Windsor at 7 o'clock Sunday morning. They

Opened in 1871, Windsor Central School was converted and used as City Hall from about 1903 through 1956. The present City Hall was built on the same site and opened in 1958. In the background is All Saints Anglican Church.

were billetted on the Janisse farm just outside the city.

Hundreds poured into the city with every passing hour; they came from the surrounding countryside by wagon, by boat, and train; others crossed by ferry from Detroit to join and congratulate their Canadian cousins on this important day.

It was a day to remember, a day marked by saturation coverage of the city's two newspapers, *The Windsor Record*, a daily and its sister, the Windsor *Weekly Record*.

In its Friday, May 27 edition, which was the first issue after the celebration, the *Weekly Record* started the story at the top left hand corner of the Front Page with a headline in bold, capital letters:

BOOM-TE-RA-RA

Our Birthday Party a hummer from hummerville

Far short of today's tabloid newspapers, to be sure, but by 19th Century standards it was stout stuff.

The story began:

"Tramp, tramp, tramp
Boom! Boom! Boom!
Did Windsor bubble over?
Well, we should say so."

In 1892 the Klondike Gold Rush was still firing the minds of fortune-seekers everywhere ... a woolen mill in Essex County discovered its own mother-lode by providing blankets for sale to those heading northwest in search of wealth beyond imagining.

The *Weekly Record*, then owned by McNee and McKay, and selling for $1 per annum (in advance), had recently reported the launching of a "fine ferry boat built for the Detroit, Belle Isle and Windsor Ferry Company."

"No person ever suspected that the citizens of Windsor had so much enthusiasm concealed about their clothes ... She is not often affected that way, but she had it yesterday ... Everybody — well

Bartlet & Macdonald, later Bartlet, Macdonald & Gow, an important department store, was located at Ouellette Avenue and Sandwich Street (now Riverside Drive).

nearly everybody — took a lively hand."

Electric street lighting arrived in 1890, the same year that the first patient was admitted to Hotel Dieu Hospital.

"The citizens took right hold and nearly every building in the city was gay with bunting and flags. The Trades and Society Procession was simply immense and the spirits of the people present were away up ..."

Windsor's first telephone exchange came in 1880 and by 1892, there were 205 subscribers. By 1888 the city had three miles of paved streets and in 1891 council voted to spend $20,000 on paving. In June 1886 the first commercial electric railway system in Canada started running between Windsor and Walkerville ...

"The procession occupied over an hour in passing a given place ... About 9 o'clock in the morning people began moving towards the rendezvous for the procession at the corner of Bruce Avenue and Sandwich Street. Shortly after 10 o'clock the procession got a move on ..."

Cod liver oil sold at 35 cents a bottle and was said to be good for those suffering from difficulty of breathing, tightness of chest, wasting away of flesh, throat troubles, bronchitis, weak lungs, asthma, coughs, catarrh and colds.

Pickles were selling 20 to 30 cents per hundred; potatoes, 45 cents per bushel; dressed chicken, 6 cents per pound.

"Immediately after dinner the crowd wended its way to the park and during the afternoon, from Sandwich Street to the park, Ouellette Avenue was a veritable living mass of humanity ...

"The crowd was immense and exceeded all expectations. Only a small portion of the number visited the park, yet that was filled to overflowing ..."

Canada's population was 4,833,000 in 1891 ... the Canadian West was opening to settlers ... the CPR advertised trains leaving

Horse races, band performances and other community events were held at the Driving Park, now Jackson Park.

... But Not Without Dissention

How much is local talent worth to a proud and growing community ready to celebrate its coming of age as a city?

On Sunday, May 8, 1892, only 16 days before the celebration to mark Windsor's incorporation, a public meeting was called to outline final plans and announce that Council had set aside $1,000 to help pay for the party. This included something to cover expenses incurred by local companies of the 21st Fusiliers, who had been invited to march in the parade along with the famed Toronto Grenadiers.

James Anderson, a member of the General Committee which was responsible for organizing the event, felt that was an unnecessary extravagance. Minutes of General Committee meetings quoted Anderson as saying the city should not bear the expenses of the hometown Fusiliers.

He argued that the Toronto Grenadiers were the main military attraction and that the Fusiliers would want to participate with or without compensation.

His proposal was lost under what was described as "a spirited defence by Capt. Reeves ..." another member of the General Committee.

The Weekly Record devoted its May 27 front page to a detailed report of the new city's inaugural celebration.

Toronto every Tuesday for Manitoba and the Northwest.

"At 12 o'clock the celebration committee banquetted the visitors and officers at the British American (Hotel). A large number sat down to a good spread ...

"General Committee Chairman Francis Cleary proposed the toasts to the Queen and Dominion and Provincial Parliaments ... Immediately after the banquet the party took hacks and proceeded to the Driving Park (Jackson Park) to see the sports and military display ..."

The Evening Record is two years old ... it is a pretty feisty infant ... The roads between Windsor and Amherstburg have been improved so that the stage can be used again ...

"Shortly after 3 o'clock the Grenadiers and Fusiliers headed by their respective bands arrived at the Driving Park and took up positions preparatory to the Grenadiers going through the movements of trooping the colours ... After the trooping of the colours the Grenadiers and Fusiliers returned to the city."

The three cars on the Sandwich line cover 462 metres per day ... The demand for lights is so great that the Citizens Electric Light Company will install a new 1800 candlepower dynamo ...

In April, the Ontario Legislature passed, with a one-vote majority, a new bill allowing women to study and practise law in the province.

"Before the train pulled out, Col. Dawson attempted to make a speech but the noise of the assembled was too great and beyond a few in his immediate vicinity, his remarks were unheard."

Biff
　　Bang
　　　　Boom!
Oh what a jag.
Take in your flags.
It was a hummer
Didn't we spread ourselves ... ?

(Sources: 49, 54)

The Beeman House, one of Windsor's earliest hotels, opened in 1855 at the northeast corner of Pitt Street and Ouellette Avenue.

James Casimir Guillot (above and right) was a Major in the 21st Essex Fusiliers at the inaugural celebration. The following year, he was appointed City Treasurer.

Party Time In '92

THE QUEEN AND THE ROYAL FAMILY.

THE QUEEN.—Victoria, of the United Kingdom of Great Britain and Ireland, Queen, Empress of India, Defender of the Faith. Her Majesty was born at Kensington Palace, May 24, 1819; succeeded to the throne June 20, 1837, on the death of her uncle King William IV.; was crowned June 28, 1838, and married Feb. 10, 1840, to His Royal Highness Prince Albert. Her Majesty is the only child of his late Royal Highness Edward, Duke of Kent, son of George III. The children of Her Majesty are—

Her Royal Highness Victoria Adelaide Mary Louisa, PRINCESS ROYAL OF ENGLAND AND PRUSSIA, born Nov. 21, 1840, and married to the late Emperor Frederick of Germany, Jan. 25, 1858, and has issue four sons and four daughters.

His Royal Highness Albert Edward, PRINCE OF WALES, born Nov. 9, 1841; married March 10, 1863, Alexandra of Denmark, (Princess of Wales), born Dec. 1, 1844, and has issue, Prince Albert Victor, born Jan. 8, 1864 (died 1892); George Frederick Ernest Albert, born June 3, 1865; Louisa Victoria Alexandra Dagmar, born Feb. 20, 1867; Victoria Alexandra Olga Mary, born July 6, 1868; and Maude Charlotte Mary Victoria, born Nov. 26, 1869.

His Royal Highness Alfred Ernest Albert Duke of Edinburgh, born Aug. 6, 1844; married Her Imperial Highness the Grand Duchess Marie of Russia, Jan. 23, 1874, and has issue one son and five daughters.

Her Royal Highness Helen Augusta Victoria, born May 25, 1846; married to H. R. H. Prince Frederick Christian Charles Augustus of Schleswig-Holenstein-Sonderburg-Augustenburg, July 5, 1866, and has issue 3 sons and 2 daughters.

Her Royal Highness Louisa Carolina Alberta, born March 18, 1848; married to the Marquis of Lorne, March 2, 1871.

His Royal Highness Arthur William Patrick Albert, Duke of Connaught, born May 1, 1850; married March 13, 1879, to Princess Louise Margaret, daughter of Prince Frederick Charles of Prussia, and has issue one son and two daughters.

His Royal Highness Leopold George Duncan Albert, Duke of Albany, born April 7, 1853; married April 27, 1882, to Princess Helen of Wardleck, (deceased), and has issue one son and one daughter. Died March 24, 1884.

Her Royal Highness Beatrice, Mary Victoria Feudore, born April 14, 1857; married July 23, 1885 to Prince Henry of Battenburg, and has issue one son and one daughter.

Her Royal Highness Alice Maud Mary, born April 25, 1843, (deceased.) Married to H. R. H. Prince Frederick Louis of Hesse, July 1, 1862, and had issue five daughters and two sons; second son killed by accident May, 1873. Died December 14th, 1878.

WINDSOR CITY COUNCIL, 1892.

MAYOR, O. E. FLEMING; ALDERMEN—S. T. REEVES, JAMES SHEPHERD, JOHN HARMAN, NEIL REAUME, JOHN T. WEAR, A. F. NASH, E. W. S. BAUER, T. W. BROOKE, R. LAMBERT, DR. J. A. SMITH, P. A. BARNES, JOSEPH MARTIN.

THE CITY OF WINDSOR.

WINDSOR, the Canadian City of the Straits, which is now (May 24th, 1892) celebrating its erection into a city, occupies historic ground. Situated on the greatest water highway of this continent, it was early visited by the devout French missionaries and the energetic French voyageur and trader.

As early as the spring of 1670 the missionaries, Galinee and Dollier, ascended the Detroit River, and on the 11th of August, 1679, the intrepid La Salle entered the Detroit River with his vessel, the Griffin, a forty-five-ton craft, and the forerunner of that magnificent fleet of vessels which now navigate these inland waters.

In a short sketch, such as can be given in the space at our disposal, it is not possible to relate the early struggles of the settlers along the Detroit River on the present site of Windsor, or in its vicinity. This section is rich is romance and adventure. Volumes could be written of the conflicts between the soldiers of England and of France, and between the red man and the white. Many heroic

Games, Races and Amusements.

Tuesday, May 24th, 1892,

10 a. m.:—Military, Trades and Society parade, through the principal streets of the City.

11 a. m.:—Foot Ball Tournament on Ouellette Square.

2 p. m:—Trooping of Military Colors at the Driving Park. The 10th Royal Grenadiers, the 21st Fusiliers and the Cavalry will take part.

3 p. m.:—Athletic Sports at the Driving Park.

A 24-page programme booklet was produced by The Evening Record as a guide to the celebration of Windsor's birth as a city. These pages are reproduced courtesy of the Hiram Walker Historical Museum.

Part Two:

The Early Years

A Time Of Birth, Growth And Glory

Pen and ink sketch of Our Lady of Assumption Church.

CITY OF WINDSOR (WACAC)/ARTIST: BYRON LEE

The story of the founding of Assumption Parish (L'Assomption) in 1767 is more than just another story about the beginning of another Catholic church in the wilderness of Upper Canada . . .

It is more than just another story about a God-loving, black-robed Jesuit missionary priest tending to the spiritual needs of his flock on a small spit of land in the Detroit River Region . . .

The story of the founding of Assumption is really a rich saga of the beginning of a province: it was here in the mid-18th Century, during the French Period, that Ontario was born — a fact of history that has been largely overlooked, downplayed, or simply ignored over the years.

But to have some comprehension of the embryonic events as they developed, it is necessary to go back almost 300 years, to understand why anyone would be drawn to this untamed backwoods country in the first place. Except for a handful of explorers and bush-runners, this land, 600 miles from anyplace, was unknown to the outside world. What was the challenge? You could argue that life away from the press of other business was its own reward, but it was also incredibly harsh, bitter — and even cruel.

What was the lure; what was the prize?

Some of those who came did so for the sheer adventure; the challenge of going where few had gone before. For others there was a job to be done. For more than a few there was the promise of potential wealth.

Antoine de la Mothe Cadillac came in 1701 to build a fort and fur-trading post and establish a fledgling farm community. Cadillac had been commandant at Michilimackinac from 1694 to 1697 and he wanted to shift the centre of importance from the severe climate of the far north, to the shores of a clear deep river, south of Lake St. Clair where the air was caressed by warm breezes and a corn crop was assured each year. By Cadillac's reckoning, this area known as *le Detroit* (the strait) was the Eden of the Great Lakes country.

After carefully exploring the land, Cadillac decided that the north side's elevation gave his guns control of marine traffic, keeping both British and hostile Iroquois in check. The rich soil would allow a farm community to take root. He built his fort and named it Pontchartrain after Louis Phelipaux Comte de Pontchartrain, then chancellor of France.

Although Fort Pontchartrain was to be the new fur-trading centre, there were no Indian trappers to supply the furs, so Cadillac invited those at Mackinac to move south and enjoy the protection of his post. Families of Ottawa, Pottawatomi, Huron and Chippewa accepted.

Others followed:

The Jesuits, invited by friendly Hurons came to do what they did best — evangelize, convert and baptize.

The French settlers came because they were offered a chance for a new life with generous land grants, tools, food, clothing, seed and livestock.

For the first 40 years activity was concentrated on the north side of the river and the shift south didn't begin until 1742 when the missionary, Rev. Armand de la Richardie, relocated the mission from a point near the Fort, to Bois Blanc (Bob-lo) Island. Unfortunately not all Huron Indians were friendly and in 1747 marauders from Ohio destroyed the mission. Dismayed but undeterred, Father Richardie moved to within sight of the fort, on a parcel of land not far from where the present church stands.

Meanwhile, two other important changes were occurring:

(1) Responsibility for the mission was shifting from Father Richardie who had taken ill, to Father Pierre Potier, his assistant;

(2) In 1749, land grants on the south shore were being picked up by the French settlers including many with such familiar family names as Gervais, St. Louis, Drouillard, Pillette and Lafleur. While they technically belonged to Ste. Anne Parish in Detroit, many

The "Mission House" was built as a rectory for Assumption Parish in 1785. This photograph was taken about 1895.

chose to attend services in the more convenient mission chapel on this side of the river.

In 1765, 60 families petitioned for their own parish and a new church, serving both the French and the Indians, was built to replace the dilapidated chapel of 1749.

In 1767, when virtually the rest of southern Ontario was still unbroken, Father Potier became the first pastor of Our Lady of The Assumption — the first pastor of a Roman Catholic parish in

This view of Assumption Church, from a water colour by Dr. Edward Walsh in 1804, is: "A view of Detroit from the Straits, taken from the Huron Church". It was built in 1787 and the side props were added after a windstorm caused the building to lean.

what is now Ontario. Father Potier died on July 16, 1781, following a fall, at the age of 73.

Father Potier's successor, Father Francois Xavier Hubert, who arrived in November 1781, wanted to build a new church, presbytery and school, but discovered that nearly all the church property had been sold to pay outstanding debts.

On March 4, 1782, the Hurons, who had made the original land grant, agreed to give another large parcel to the parish, and construction of this, the third church, started in 1784. It was completed in 1787.

The present Assumption church was officially opened on July 20, 1846 — 11 years after work on the foundation began. It stands today, in the shadow of the Ambassador Bridge, an historic reminder that it was at this place, on the south shore of the Detroit River, that Ontario — as we know it today — had its beginning.

(Sources: 10, 11, 18, 28, 29, 35, 37, 54)

The Two Baby Houses

This is a story of two homes owned by two brothers — Jacques and François — sons of Jacques and Suzanne Baby, who were among the first of the early French pioneer families to settle on the south shore of the Detroit River in the 1760s.

It is a story of two homes whose histories are bound to the settlement of the Western District ... to the Northwest fur trade, to the War of 1812, to the Battle of Windsor in 1838.

The family name, spelled B-a-b-y, is pronounced Baw-bee.

The Duff-Baby House

Jacques Baby, appointed Inspector General in 1815, was one of the most influential men in Upper Canada.

It is no exaggeration to say that this house is reputedly the oldest surviving house in the Western District; or that it has remained relatively unchanged structurally since it was built in 1798; or that it was owned by Jacques Baby, who in his time, was one of the most influential persons in Upper Canada.

At first glance, the building seems ordinary enough: Dormers at the roof line, a full porch with steps leading to a wide expanse of lawn, a half dozen trees and shrubs ...

The house might appear ordinary looking, but its past is not.

Almost a century before Windsor became a city, Britain turned Detroit over to the Americans, and those who didn't want to live under the Stars and Stripes were offered land in what was to become the Town of Sandwich.

Among those who took the offer was Alexander Duff, a Scottish fur trader who obtained the Russell Street property with direct access to the river. It was here, in 1798, that he built his handsome Georgian home which doubled as a lucrative fur-trading establishment. In 1807 Duff sold the property to Jacques Baby, the first member of Upper Canada's French community to gain prominence in government circles. In 1792 Baby received lifetime appointments to the Executive and Legislative Councils. Although Baby was a successful merchant and also accumulated more than 22,000 acres of land, he suffered heavy losses during the

The Jacques Baby house on Mill Street in the 1890s.

MINISTRY OF CULTURE AND COMMUNICATIONS

The François Baby House

The years have not been kind to a building which, for 180 years, has stood sentinel over the most historically important homestead site in the city. The two-storey brick building is neither pretty nor imposing; it has had pieces added and subtracted with thoughtless abandon; it has been the victim of fire, storms and invading armies; it has been patched and plastered and tarted up so much that at times it looks, well ... forgotten ... overshadowed and squeezed uncomfortably on what is now a postage-stamp lot in the heart of downtown Windsor.

All that said, what remains of the site of the François Baby House is one of the last, identifiable direct links to our early settlement years. In its glory days "La Ferme", was a traditional French ribbon farm; its east-west boundaries extended from what

War of 1812 and was one of the 600 soldiers taken prisoner at the Battle of the Thames.

In 1815, as compensation for his losses and in recognition of his loyalty, he was appointed Inspector General of Upper Canada; he also became a director of the first Provincial Bank of Upper Canada, and was named Speaker of the Legislative Council.

Jacques Baby died at York (Toronto) on February 19, 1833 at the age of 70 and was buried in Sandwich's historic Assumption Church graveyard. The home, left to his eldest child, Elisabeth Ann, was bought two years later by his son, Charles, who became Mayor of Sandwich. Charles lived there with his family until 1871.

A variety of tenants occupied it until 1905 when it was bought by Dr. William Beasley, whose family held it until 1979 when the property was acquired by the Ontario Heritage Foundation. In 1990, an organization called Les Amis Duff-Baby was formed to rally support in favour of restoring it to its original condition, and to have it opened to the public as an important marker in Sandwich's historic past.

HIRAM WALKER HISTORICAL MUSEUM

Although no records exist to tell us with precision what the François Baby House originally looked like, this engraving was derived from a small drawing by Benson J. Lossing, October 6, 1860.

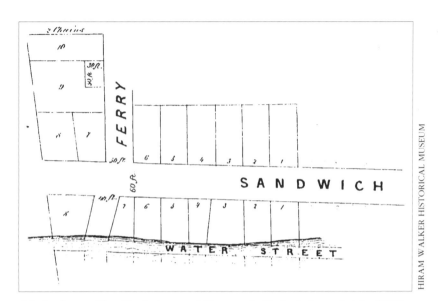

Map shows the first stage of François Baby's hamlet in 1832.

This was Stage 4 in the evolution of the François Baby House in the 1890s. It served as the base from which "Doctor Aikman" extolled the virtues of the Monroe Improved Gold Cure. (Mansion to Museum: R. Alan Douglas, 1989.)

is now Pelissier, to an alley between Bruce and Church streets and from the riverfront south to Cabana Road.

The original French homestead was established about 1760 by the patriarch, Jacques Duperon Baby, a member of one of the most influential families in the Western District. In 1790 the property was transferred to François by his widowed mother in exchange for ten shillings and a token pepper corn. Although the original family home was still standing, it was in serious need of repair and François decided to replace it with a new, grander one. Work began just before the outbreak of the War of 1812 and it was still unfinished when Hull and Brock took turns occupying it.

It is the remnant of that second structure that serves today as the Hiram Walker Historical Museum. While there are no records

to tell us with certainty what the building might have looked like when it was completed in 1812, recent sleuthing by museum Curator Alan Douglas confirms that it underwent as many as four radical changes. Curator Douglas is convinced that at no previous time did it resemble the structure that exists today.

What did exist was abandoned during the 1930s and by the mid-1940s there was little left but a blackened shell. Rehabilitation was carried out in the 1950s and on May 7, 1958 it reopened as a museum, a timeless reminder that it was this small development on a muddy lot at the end of a muddy street that led to a portion of "La Ferme" being called The Ferry, changed later to Richmond and changed again in 1836 to Windsor.

(Sources: 13, 35, 54)

The War Of 1812 Started Here

The opening gambit in the War of 1812/14 — the gambit in which a superior American army was supposed to capture Fort Malden, but ended up surrendering Detroit instead — was one of the strangest episodes of the war, and still has military strategists scratching their heads in wonder

The scene opened on July 12, 1812 when American Brigadier General William Hull's Army of the Northwest, a force of 2,000 men crossed the Detroit River, landing at what is now Walkerville. The script called for him to march downriver, past The Ferry (now Windsor) to Sandwich and continue on to capture Fort Malden at Amherstburg. Success would have provided the first American victory in the newly declared war.

But something went awry and what should have been a relatively simple military victory ended less than five weeks later in humiliating defeat for Hull.

Looking back, it seems that while as many things went wrong as went right for the Americans, several factors shifted the balance:

(1) Commander of His Britannic Majesty's force was the impetuous, seasoned, professional Major General Isaac Brock, a skilled military strategist with the nerve of a riverboat gambler. One biographer described Brock as tall, stout and inclining to corpulency; he was of fair and florid complexion, had a large forehead, full face, small, greyish eyes, with a very slight cast in one of them; small mouth with pleasing smile and good teeth. He was exceedingly affable and gentlemanly, partial to dancing and although never married, extremely devoted to female society.

(2) Offering him full support was the Shawnee chief Tecumseh, a persuasive orator who was able to win, for Brock, the allegiance of hundreds (perhaps thousands) of Indian braves from a variety of tribes — all anxious to distinguish themselves in battle, all enemies of the Americans. For 19th Century frontier Americans, thought of falling into the hands of warring Indians was as traumatizing as germ warfare is today — a powerful psychological tool working in Brock's favour.

Four paintings, including this one and another on Page 27, depicting aspects of the War of 1812 were commissioned about 1973 from John C. Forster, a Windsor artist. This one, titled "Tecumseh and Brock Meet at Bois Blanc", recalls their first meeting before launching a successful counter-attack on Detroit. Amherstburg can be seen across the river.

W.R. (BILL) RANSOME COLLECTION

(3) The American army was largely composed of untrained, undisciplined militia, ready to defend their country but reluctant to fight on foreign soil. Leading them was tobacco-chewing General Hull, governor of the Michigan Territory. Although Hull had distinguished himself during the Revolutionary War he had accepted this task reluctantly ... was past his military prime ... and

1. Two thousand American troops landed roughly where the Hiram Walker distillery complex is today.
2. General William Hull marches downstream, establishing field camp at the François Baby farm where Hiram Walker Historical Museum stands today.
3. Town of Sandwich.
4. British hold back American invaders at River Canard.
5. Hull fails to capture Fort Malden.
6. Brock and Tecumseh land at Spring Wells on their way to capture Detroit.

apparently incapable of directing such a large offensive. Among his officers was his own son, Captain Abraham Hull whose drinking habits lost him whatever shreds of respect his men had for him when, one day in a drunken stupor, he toppled from his horse while crossing a river during manoeuvres.

Although the outcome of the struggle for Malden was crucial in that its capture could have opened the door to American control of Upper Canada, a chronology of events suggests that what began with the wide-screen solemnity of Ben Hur, ended in a frenzy reminiscent of a Keystone Kops movie.

SUNDAY, JULY, 12, 1812

Hull sends a decoy contingent downstream from Detroit while his main force crosses upstream, landing where the Hiram Walker complex now stands on Riverside Drive. Col. Lewis Cass a professional soldier anxious to make war, is the first to leap ashore and unfurl the Stars and Stripes on Canadian soil. Hull marches downstream a few miles to establish his headquarters on the François Baby farm, directly opposite Detroit.

TUESDAY, JULY 14, 1812

Hull fortifies his Baby house defences with a breastwork around three inland sides and mounts artillery on the fourth, facing Detroit, giving him full control of the river.

THURSDAY, JULY 16 to MONDAY, JULY 20, 1812

Hull tests the British defences with a series of skirmishes at a bridge over the River Canard, between Sandwich and Amherstburg.

SATURDAY, JULY 25, 1812

An American patrol retreats to the Baby farm after being ambushed at Turkey Creek.

FRIDAY, AUGUST 7, 1812

Hull learns that Brock and Tecumseh, leading hundreds of Indian warriors, are approaching Fort Malden. Fearing that he has left Detroit vulnerable, Hull and his men return to Detroit.

THURSDAY, AUGUST 13, 1812

Brock and Tecumseh arrive at the now-abandoned Baby farm. Royal Engineers install gun emplacements, some hidden behind the walls of the original Baby home, others concealed in a creek

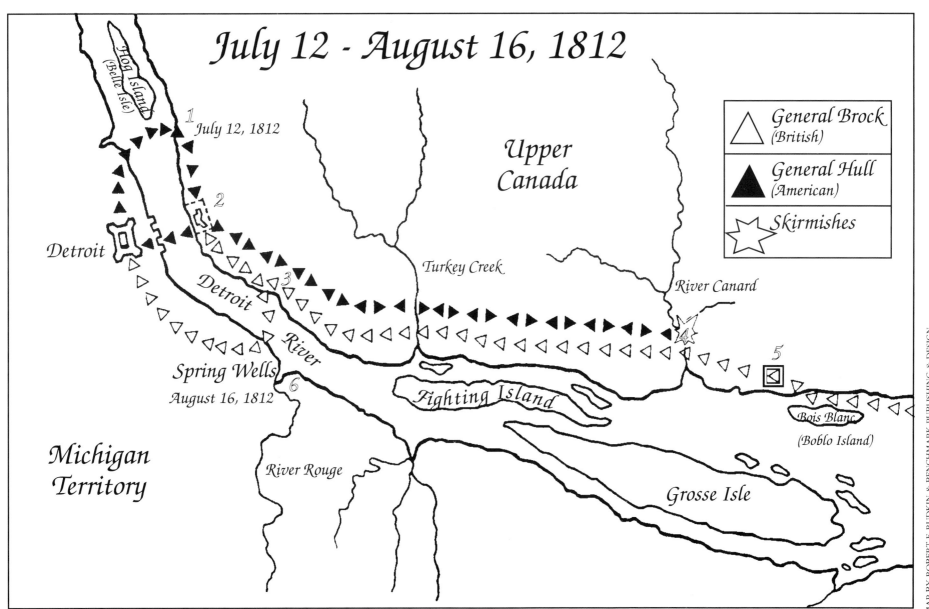

July 12 - August 16, 1812

Hog Island (Belle Isle)

1 July 12, 1812

2

Upper Canada

Detroit

Detroit River

Turkey Creek

3

River Canard

4

General Brock (British)

General Hull (American)

Skirmishes

5

Spring Wells

August 16, 1812

6

Fighting Island

Bois Blanc (Boblo Island)

Michigan Territory

River Rouge

Grosse Isle

MAP BY ROBERT F. RUDKIN & BENCHMARK PUBLISHING & DESIGN

bed. The growing Indian support includes Ottawas, Chippewas, Wyandottes, Pottawatomies, Miamis, Shawnees, Sacs, Foxes, Kickapoos, Winnebagoes and Dacotahs.

FRIDAY, AUGUST 14, 1812

Brock sends a message to Hull ordering him to surrender; Hull refuses.

SATURDAY, AUGUST 15, 1812

The British reveal the strength of their armament:12 $\frac{1}{2}$, 18 and 24-pound cannons plus mortars. Brock begins the bombardment creating confusion inside the fort which is packed with troops, civilians, horses, equipment and livestock.

SUNDAY, AUGUST 16, 1812

At six a.m. the British open the second day of the cannonade; Many of the 600 Indians have already landed on the American shore and now, 400 militia and 300 British regulars embark in boats, canoes and barges; working downstream in full view of the fort, they land below Detroit at a point called Spring Wells. Tecumseh's followers fill the air with mind-freezing war whoops and an intimidating volley of rifle fire as they circle towards the palisades.

Brock in scarlet tunic, cocked hat and gold epaulets and Tecumseh in fringed buckskin, both mounted, would be easy targets for the American long guns as they lead disciplined columns toward Detroit. Ahead sits a battery of 24-pounders aimed straight down their throats. The colonel in charge of the gun crew swears that his fuse was ready and with one discharge, could have blown Brock back to Sandwich. He is told not to fire.

Sensing the moment, Brock repeats the earlier order to surrender. Presently, Hull's son, Captain Abraham Hull, emerges carrying a truce flag to negotiate terms of surrender which will include: the territory of Michigan, 40 barrels of powder, 400 rounds of 24-pound shot, 100,000 ball cartridges, 2500 stand-of-arms, 35 iron and eight brass cannon, a large supply of provisions, and a force of 2,500 men — twice the size of Brock's.

Not a drop of British blood has been shed.

EPILOGUE

• The War continued until Christmas Eve, 1814 when The Treaty of Ghent was signed, restoring the "status quo ante-bellum": In plain terms, everything would revert to where it had been before Hull crossed the river in an unsuccessful strike to take Fort Malden;
• Brock died in the Battle of Queenston Heights, October 13, 1812;
• Tecumseh died in the Battle of Moraviantown on October 6, 1813;
• Hull was charged with treason, cowardice, unofficer-like conduct and neglect of duty. He was found guilty on all but the charge of treason and sentenced to death by a firing squad. The death sentence was remitted by President Madison in recognition of Hull's bravery in the Revolutionary War.

(Sources: 3, 11, 14, 18, 24, 28, 30, 39, 43)

To stop the advance of invading Americans on Fort Malden, British troops destroyed the bridge at River Canard and set up breastwork defences. It was at this point that John Dean was wounded and James Hancock killed. ("Skirmish at the River Canard" is reproduced courtesy Canadian Parks Services: Fort Malden National Historic Sites.)

Dean And Hancock: Two Names To Remember

In almost any country — other than Canada — where wars and warriors are exalted, the names of two British soldiers, privates John Dean and James Hancock, members of the 41st Regiment during the War of 1812, would be writ large in the history books, their images cast in bronze. In Canada we tend to consign memories of such important human dramas to the small-print footnotes of history.

In almost any other country, school children would bring their history lessons to life by reciting, for the umpteenth time, the heroic tale of how Dean and Hancock defended Fort Malden by holding their ground at the bridge over River Canard against the advancing American army — becoming the first troops — British or American, to shed blood on Canadian soil in the War of 1812.

They would tell how, on July 16, Private Dean, one arm broken by a musket shot, held off the invaders with his bayonet until he was bowled over and taken prisoner ... of how Private Hancock, also wounded, sank to his knees and was finally overrun, his body mutilated by bayonet thrusts.

(Sources: 3, 38)

Folklore has it that the meeting to pick the name Windsor was held in this hotel, previously called Hutton's Tavern, and that it was renamed Windsor Castle in celebration of the occasion. More recent information, however, suggests that while the meeting was probably held in this building, its identification as Hutton's might be inaccurate.

September 6, 1836 – The Day They Named It Windsor

You could argue about whether it should be called a hamlet or a village By any name, it was a random collection of log cabins and clap-board houses overlooking what Lieutenant-Governor John Graves Simcoe once referred to as the *"Streights of Detroit".*

Geographically it was little more than a smudge on a tattered map, opposite Detroit; a faint tick-mark against the vast forests in the far reaches of the Western District of Upper Canada. But to 200 souls, it was home.

For years, there was little agreement as to what "home" should be called — officially. Not that there was a shortage of names; the greater problem was that there were too many and the boundaries were uncertain.

At different times and different places, people called it: Richmond ... Sandwich Ferry ... the South Shore ... South Detroit ... and even, the Ferry opposite Detroit.

Although villagers were clearly divided about the name, there was agreement that it was time to settle the question, time to pick a name they could call their own. A meeting to do that was called for Tuesday, September 6, 1836.

Unfortunately, fact and romantic folklore clash at this point. While we know that such a meeting was held, and that it might have been held at a tavern, the questions of who owned the tavern and what took place during and after the meeting remain unresolved.

The most popular tale says that the meeting took place in Hutton's Tavern, and soon after the name *Windsor* was selected, Mr. Hutton decided to mark the occasion by renaming the tavern Windsor Castle.

The flaw is that although an early photograph shows that a hotel with the name Windsor Castle did exist, licence records say that Mr. Hutton wasn't the proprietor — and that he probably didn't come to town until sometime between 1842 and 1846.

Although we can't know for sure what took place at that meeting, there is room for historical conjecture which suggests that besides the variety of names then in current usage, the villagers also considered three others: Bellevue, Montpelier and Babylon — a play on the Baby family name.

Speculation by the late Windsor historical researcher, George F. Macdonald, is that the list was quickly pared to two — Richmond and South Detroit. Mr. Macdonald, who spent most of his adult life delving into Windsor's past, argues that Robert Mercer and Joseph McDougall, two of the community's prominent citizens, would each have favoured one of those names for personal reasons. Because of that, their supporters at the meeting would have been in a deadlock that could have been broken only by a third party — James Dougall, a merchant, who suggested *Windsor*. Logic has

it that that name would have been acceptable for two important reasons: not only was it neutral, but it also had a comfortable, "back-home" familiarity.

The Canadian Emigrant, the first newspaper published in Sandwich, carried this report on September 13, 1836:

"The meeting for the purpose of naming the village at the ferry, in the 6th instant, resulted in its being called 'Windsor.'"

Call it what you want, The Emigrant was ready to sing its praises under any name. Mr. Macdonald culled the following journalistic gem from the February 21, 1835 edition of the paper:

"It is a pleasing duty to notice the improvements which have been made in a short time in the vicinity of the Ferry. But a few months since and the traveller could only discover the place by finding himself opposite the city of Detroit, and if he happened to be an Eastern Patriarch journeying with his flocks and herds, wives and little ones

Variety Of Early Names Did Not Include "Windsor"

By the time the citizens got around to deciding that this necklace of homes and shops strung out along the Detroit River should be called *Windsor*, at least eight names were being used — but Windsor was not among them.

They included:

Richmond	L'Assomption Settlement
The Ferry	The Ferry opposite Detroit
Sandwich Ferry	Sandwich Ferry opposite Detroit
South Detroit	The South Side

Considering that there had been continued, though slow, growth for at least 25 years, why it took so long to pick a name remains a mystery.

Still, the decision was timely enough. By 1832 there were signs that some form of community planning was taking place. That year François Baby hired Thomas Smith, a Welsh-born surveyor, living in Petite Cote (LaSalle), to design a subdivision in the area generally known as Sandwich Ferry and then Richmond.

On August 6, the first urban lot in what was to become Windsor was sold to James Austen, a wagon-maker. The lot was located at the southeast corner of what is now Riverside Drive and Ferry Street.

In 1835 Joseph McDougall laid out a second subdivision further to the east which he called South Detroit.

James Dougall, community leader and owner of this dry goods store, favoured "Windsor" over "South Detroit" or "Richmond".

from the land of steady habits to the Canaan of Michigan, it were doubtful if he could procure lodging for the night. Now his pilgrimage draws to an end in a flourishing town, and his heart is cheered with the promise of good fare by the sight of good taverns and handsome accommodations."

Mr. Macdonald's searching also led him to what is believed to be the first known public use of the name Windsor. It was used in an advertisement for goods and appeared in the November 16, 1836 edition of The Emigrant.

It featured household goods and hardware of all kinds and was signed:

J & J Dougall.
Windsor, opposite Detroit, 14th September, 1836

(Sources: 11, 32, 52, 54)

Barbarism And The Battle Of Windsor

The cryptic message on the plaque outside the Hiram Walker Historical Museum, describing the Battle of Windsor in 1838, is a marvel of historic understatement.

"Early on December 4, 1838, a force of about 140 American and Canadian supporters of William Lyon Mackenzie crossed from Detroit and landed about one mile east of here. After capturing and burning a militia barracks they took possession of Windsor ... They were routed by a force of about 130 militiamen commanded by Col. John Prince. Five of the invaders were taken prisoner and executed by order of Col. Prince. This caused violent controversy in Canada and The United States. The remaining captives were tried and sentenced ... Six were executed, eighteen transported to a penal colony in Tasmania and sixteen deported."

The summary is accurate but it falls yards short of telling the incredibly colourful story and the stormy aftermath of this episodic shoot-out that lasted less than 24 hours, left 31 dead, 40 captured; led to two public horsewhippings, a pistol duel — and triggered a political rhubarb that echoed all the way to the hallowed chambers of the House of Lords in London, England.

Of the 31 dead, 27 were invaders, five of whom were executed on the spot at Prince's orders. Four were Windsor defenders including Dr. John Hume, who was found hiding in a large cask. He was dragged out, bayonetted, hacked with an axe, robbed and, according to at least one account, his body was left for the hogs to mutilate.

That act of barbarism led Prince to order the executions which were met with cries of shame. Not one to take criticism lightly, Prince horsewhipped two of his critics, fought and won a pistol duel and saw to the demotion of some of his officers.

When a dead-or-alive bounty for Prince was offered he protected his property with 12, spring-loaded guns and man-traps. In the end he won every challenge, civil or military, physical or legal, and the invaders never returned.

Hot-tempered Col. John Prince tolerated no insults.

The Battle of Windsor was not a "battle" in the sense that there was a declaration of war, rather it was barely more than a scruffy little turf war, one of a series of privately mounted attacks on Canadian territory following the aborted 1837 Mackenzie/Papineau Rebellion of Upper and Lower Canada. Although the invaders fancied themselves "Patriots", with a mission to impose American democracy in Canada (opponents called it mobocracy), Prince saw them as a gang of ne'er-do-well Americans and expatriate Canadians looking for adventure and loot. He mocked them as

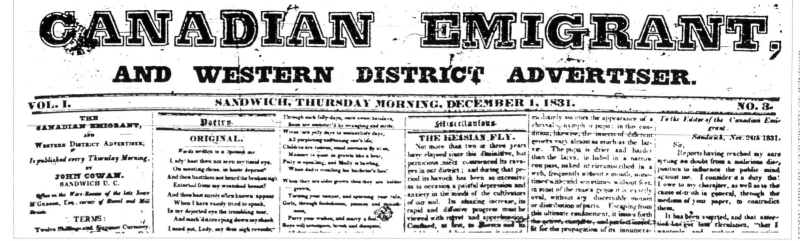

The Canadian Emigrant, and Western District Advertiser, established in 1831, was the first newspaper to serve the Border Towns.

pirates and bandits, and defended his frontier justice by arguing the captives were not prisoners of war because there was no war.

The surprise attack began early Tuesday morning, December 4, 1838 when the invaders boarded the steamboat *Champlain* in Detroit and landed upstream on the Canadian side, almost where General William Hull did in 1812. On their march downstream to Windsor, they wounded a sentry at the barracks, burned the guardhouse, killed the owner of a farmhouse and torched the steamer *Thames*, before overrunning the François Baby house.

By six in the morning, Windsor was in enemy hands — but the victory was short-lived. Within 30 minutes, church bells were clanging and an alarm gun was fired in Sandwich as five militia companies marched to meet the invaders. Prince, who arrived wearing a hunting costume, fur cap, shooting jacket and sword, quickly learned of his doctor friend's fate. Outraged by this act of barbarism, and having considered the shortage of jail facilities and the fact that regular army reinforcements had not arrived, Prince decided to take direct action. He said later:

"I therefore resolved upon shooting at once and without a moment's hesitation, every bandit that happened to be captured and brought in."

Prince's supporters and opponents were divided and vocal. Newspapers took sides, but most congratulated him as his fame spread across the country. In February, 1839, the Western Herald supported Prince editorially and in angry response, nine community leaders cancelled their subscriptions. Prince challenged one of them, William R. Wood, deputy clerk of the peace, to a duel and in a diary entry said:

"Distance twelve paces. At the first shots my pistol missed fire. On the second shot I hit Mr. Wood in the jaw and the ball lodged there. He missed both shots. Home by eight to breakfast. I sent him home in my sleigh and Rudyerd (Prince's second) and I walked all the way."

Public debate see-sawed furiously throughout the spring and summer until finally, on September 21, 1839, a committee of arbitrators encouraged all "to be unreservedly willing to express their unfeigned regret at what has unfortunately taken place."

Common sense prevailed, the chapter was closed and the loaded spring-guns, dismantled.

(Sources: 12, 35, 54)

Queen's Birthday
MAY 24, 1892.

CITY
· OF ·
WINDSOR
INAUGURATION.

Part Three:

The Changing Times

From Stagecoach To Steam Engine

W hat was life in Windsor really like in the mid years of the 19th Century? What were the people like?

While it's difficult to create mental images based on lifeless statistical charts or textbook recitations, important clues were left by such remarkable people as Anna Jameson who travelled through the backwoods of Upper Canada and later wrote about the incredible things she saw, the fascinating people she met. Anna Jameson was a noted and determined 19th Century British author who had earned a reputation as a prolific writer, a tenacious traveller and outspoken commentator even before she came to Canada. Her particular strength was her ability to write descriptively and dramatically about everyday events, adding a dash of spice to what would otherwise be a dry and bland mix of historical data.

Soon after her arrival in Toronto in December 1836, she let it be known that the following year she would travel across Upper Canada to the Detroit River, then head north to Lake Huron.

The decision horrified her new Canadian friends who deemed it madness at best. They tried, unsuccessfully, to dissuade her with predictions of certain disaster. The country, after all was still an untamed, unmapped wilderness. Certainly no place for a gentlewoman just arrived from Britain.

Ignoring the cautions, she set out, travelling in the end, where few white men and even fewer women had ever set foot. As her friends predicted, she did suffer hardship and privation — but she survived and returned home to write of her experiences.

The book that flowed from that trip, *Winter Studies and Summer Rambles in Canada* gives us an intimate and unique look at the people and the land as

Looking west along Sandwich Street from Goyeau Street to Ouellette Avenue.

Windsor's first St. Andrew's Presbyterian Church was built in 1865 and replaced by the present structure in 1883.

she journeyed for weeks on end by wagon, coach, steamship — and even by log canoe.

After arriving in Detroit she took ill, and while recuperating, found time to visit what she described as the "little hamlet opposite to Detroit", referring to it as *"Richmond"* even though the name *"Windsor"* had been officially adopted just the year before.

Her brief visit produced an interesting perspective:

"I hardly know how to convey to you an idea of the difference between the two shores it will appear to you as incredible as it is to me incomprehensible.

"Our shore is said to be the more fertile but to float between them (as I did today in a little canoe made of a hollow tree, and paddled by a half-breed imp of a boy) to behold on one side, a city, with its towers and spires and animated population, with villas and handsome houses stretching along the shore, and a hundred vessels or more, gigantic steamers, brigs, schooners, crowding the port, loading and unloading; all the bustle, in short, of prosperity and commerce; and on the other side, a struggling hamlet, one schooner, one little wretched steamboat, some windmills, a Catholic chapel or two, a supine ignorant peasantry, all the symptoms of apathy, indolence, mistrust, hopelessness!

Can I, can anyone, help wondering at the difference and asking whence it arises?"

(*Sources: 25*)

RICHMOND - 1835
LATER WINDSOR, ONTARIO

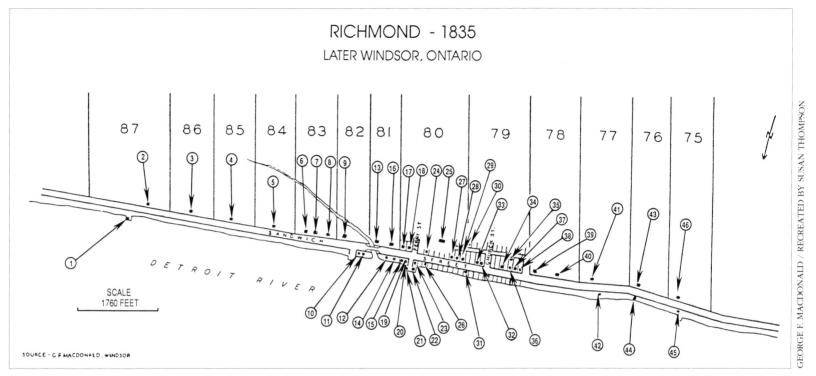

This 1835 map of Richmond was in a presentation "How Windsor Got its Name" by historian George F. Macdonald at the annual meeting of the Essex Historical Society on January 21, 1921. Mr. Macdonald said that Richmond began at what is now Glengarry Avenue on the east and extended west to what is now Crawford Avenue.

1. Store, warehouse and forwarding establishment of Messrs. Verhoeff and Jasperson
2. Dwelling house of Mr. Jasperson
3. Residence of Robert Mercer, Esq.
4. Dwelling, the property of Mr. Joseph McDougall
5. Dwelling of Mr. Pratt
6. Dwelling of Mr. Lee
7. Dwelling of Mr. Daniel Goyeau
8. Store of Mr. James Charles
9. Store of Mr. Morin & Co.
10. St. Amour's tavern and ferry
11. Dwelling of widow St. Amour
12. Shoe shop of Mr. Brown
13. Dwelling of Mr. Ouellette
14. New and splendid Mansion House, by Mr. Jos. House
15. Pavilion House, by Messrs. Murray and Crawford
16. Tin, Copper and Sheet Iron Factory and residence of Mr. House
17. Wagon Shop of Mr. James Austin
18. Wagon Shop of Mr. James Austin
19. Grocery and provision store of Messrs. L. and H. Davenport
20. Tailor shop of Mr. Ask
21. Tailor shop of Mr. John Perry
22. The Ferry
23. Store, warehouse, wharf and forwarding establishment of Messrs. J. and J. Dougall
24. Dwelling of Mr. James Dougall
25. Dwelling of François Baby, Esq.
26. New bake house
27. Crown and Anchor Tavern by Mr. Mason
28. New building of Mr. Ask
29. New building of Mr. Wm. Moore
30. Dwelling of Mr. Wm. Johnston
31. Brewery and dwelling of Messrs. Kennedy
32. Blacksmith shop of Mr. Sowden
33. Dwelling of Mr. Sowden
34. Dwelling of Mr. Pickhard
35. Upholstery of Mr. Thomas Cole
36. Dwelling of Mr. Cole
37. Bakery of Mr. Robinson
38. Cabinet warehouse of Mr. Mason
39. Saddlery shop of Mr. Brown
40. Residence of Mr. Janette Sr.
41. Residence of Mr. Normandie
42. The Pig and Tinder Box tavern and Ferry, Leblaine's old stand, now run by Ferry Master McLean
43. Residence of Mr. N.A. Janette
44. Store house of Mr. N. A. Janette
45. Store, warehouse, wharf and forwarding establishment of J. G. Watson
46. Residence of John G. Watson

Thousands Of Black Slaves Find Freedom On Canadian Shores

They came first by the dozens, then the hundreds, then the thousands. They came from the slave states of the deep South and their single-minded goal was to escape the oppression that was their stock in life, and taste something they could only dream about — freedom. They were told that freedom could be theirs in a land called Canada.

While there are no statistics to tell us with certainty how many made it to this country, the figures 35,000 to 40,000 are commonly used. Whatever number, there's little doubt that thousands experienced their first heady taste of that freedom on the Canadian banks of the Detroit River.

But Windsor and Sandwich were more than end-of-the-line terminals, they were also important transfer points for those seeking greater security inland — beyond the reach of slave-catchers. Some moved on to Dawn, Buxton, Chatham, London and Toronto; others found our climate appealing and built homes in Amherstburg, Harrow, Puce, Malden, Colchester South and Anderdon.

Although new laws made it illegal for people in Upper Canada to acquire new slaves after 1790, the freedom message wasn't widely known until the end of the War of 1812. Even then the migration began slowly, almost hesitantly and didn't gain full momentum until 1850 when the U.S. passed the scandalous Fugitive Slave Act which gave bounty-hunters sweeping powers to round up fugitive blacks anywhere in the U.S.

With few exceptions, those who made it were hungry, uneducated and dirt-poor. They were the hunted and the haunted, travelling hundreds of miles mostly at night along winding wagon trails, across farm fields, over mountains, through swamp and forest; they came on foot, by wagon, and even packed in wooden crates and shipped by train as freight. The journey was an unbroken nightmare of uncertainty and fear. The price of failure was unthinkable.

Although some miraculously found their way virtually un-

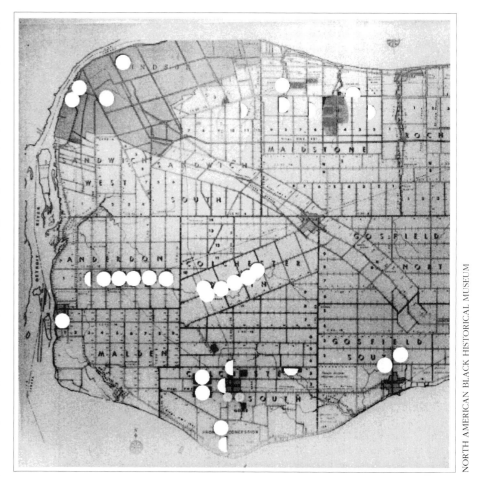

Map of the western portion of Essex County showing where early black settlements were concentrated in the 1800s.

THE · DETROIT · & · WINDSOR · FERRY · CO. · 1858.
· STR: GEM: CAP'T.: TOM · CHILVERS: Wm CAMPBELL · OWNER.

The Gem, *captained by Tom Chilver, a white abolitionist, made night runs from Detroit to Windsor carrying fugitive slaves on the last leg of their flights to freedom. Among them was a group of 12 — 11 of whom had been "kidnapped" from Southern slave dealers by John Brown, an avowed abolitionist. He spirited them away only days before they were to be sold at auction. Along the way, a baby boy was born and the mother called him Captain John Brown.*

Log house, built and lived in by John Freeman Walls, an escaped black slave, and his white wife, Jane, who fled to Canada with him, is probably the oldest black home still existing in Essex County. It is located on a 25-acre lot on Puce River in Colchester Township, bought from the Refugee Home Society in 1846.

CARL MORGAN

aided, most travelled the "Underground Railroad", the ingenious creation of a loosely knit group of abolitionists, mostly white Methodists and Quakers. This unique "railroad" had no rail lines, no rolling stock but it did have "conductors" and "station masters" who moved their "passengers" along secret routes from such slave states as Tennessee, Virginia, Missouri and Mississippi. Once on Canadian soil the fugitives became "new arrivals" and abolitionist newpapers gleefully reported their numbers and origin.

Such stories are legion and the hardships challenge the imagination.

Of all the "new arrivals", without doubt, the most unusual were John Freeman Walls, a black slave and his white wife, Jane, with her four white children. Jane was the widow of Daniel Walls, a white plantation owner in North Carolina. John Freeman Walls was one of the plantation slaves. Coincidentally, John and Daniel were born at the same time and were raised together, becoming fast friends. As was customary, John took the surname of his slaveowner. On his deathbed, Daniel asked John to care for his wife and family after he died.

Three months later, John and Jane who were in love, but knew that marriage would cost them their lives, decided to make a run for Canada. Their long and terrifying journey ended in Toledo, Ohio where they boarded the *"Pearl",* a ferry boat operated by a sympathetic, abolitionist captain, for the last leg of their perilous freedom flight.

They touched Canadian soil in Amherstburg and later made their way to Sandwich and Windsor looking for a place to settle. They decided that both places were too close to the American border for peace of mind. In 1846 they bought land in Colchester Township from the Refugee Home Society and built a log cabin on what is now the Puce Road. The original homesite has been preserved and has recently been turned into the John Freeman Walls Museum, operated by descendants of John and Jane Walls.

Again, because of imprecise records, it's impossible to say exactly how many blacks eventually settled in the Border Region. It is known, however, that by 1859, a year after Windsor became a town, the general population stood at between 2,500 and 3,000, and a visitor estimated that 700 to 800 of those were black. Most lived on what was then the eastern edge of the town; McDougall, Assumption, Pitt and Goyeau Streets. They included such trades-people as barbers, coopers, blacksmiths, shoemakers, masons, sailors and gardeners.

One of the most prominent 19th-Century blacks in the area was Delos Rogest Davis. Born in 1846, in Colchester North he became Canada's first black lawyer in May, 1885. In 1910 he became the first black lawyer to be appointed King's Counsel. James L. Dunn, who arrived in Windsor with his family in 1864 established the Dunn Varnish Works and supplied material to Massey Harris Company. He also owned a liquor store on Sandwich Street and served as a Windsor councillor in the late 1880s.

Military records show that the blacks played a role during the Rebellion of 1837-38. From December 29, 1837 to January 26, 1838, a company of black volunteers drawn from Windsor, Sandwich

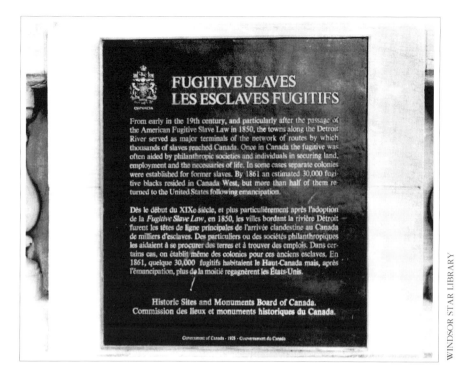

Commemorative plaque is on the east wall of the Toronto Dominion Bank Building at Riverside Drive and Ouellette Avenue.

and other parts of the county, served under Captain Caldwell at Fort Malden. Josiah Henson wrote that he was captain of the Second Company of Essex Coloured Volunteers and that he and his men assisted in the defence of Fort Malden from Christmas 1837 to May 1838.

While our laws offered freedom from slavery, they didn't offer freedom from hunger or discrimination; they didn't guarantee jobs or equality of education. Government-funded public schools were available for white students in Windsor by 1856 but black students attended a run-down rented building until 1862 when they moved into the first new — and segregated — school, St. George, at McDougall and Assumption Streets. School segregation continued in Windsor until 1888.

(Sources: 4, 6, 19, 26, 36, 46, 48, 50, 51, 54)

Masthead from the Provincial Freeman, published by Mary Ann Shadd, right.

Black Activists of the 1800s

Mary Ann Shadd, a Windsor school teacher and fiery black activist with endless energy, has to be counted as one of the most remarkably determined women of the 19th Century.

Besides being one of the first black school teachers in Windsor with a mission to wipe out segregated schools, she was also:

- The first black female newspaper editor in North America and the first female editor — black or white — in Canada;
- A lecturer and civil rights advocate at a time when that was an invitation to every form of abuse imaginable;
- At the age of 60, one of the first women to graduate as a lawyer in the U.S.

A biography said of her:

"She is tall and slim, with a fine head ... she has good features, intellectual countenance, bright sharp eyes that look right through you. She is resolute and determined and you might as well attempt to remove a stone wall with your little fingers as to check her in what she conceives to be her right and her duty."

Mary Shadd was born in Delaware in 1823 and educated in Pennsylvania. After introduction of the U.S. Fugitive Slave Act in 1850, she realized there would be a desperate need for teachers to help the poor, and largely uneducated, fugitive families arriving in Canada. Shadd joined the migration.

Arriving in Toronto in September, 1851, she attended a meeting of prominent blacks discussing common issues. Among them was Henry Bibb, a newspaper editor from Sandwich, who urged her to move to Windsor, where the need for teachers was great.

VOICE OF THE FUGITIVE

ITOR.   SANDWICH, C. W., JAN. 1, 1851.

E

degrading servitude ; but he makes no allusion to these outrages.

I will now quote, with pleasure, a sentiment in which I fully concur. The President says that ' every citizen who truly loves the Constitution, and desires the continuance of its existence and its blessing, will resolutely and firmly resist any interference in those domestic affairs which the Constitution has clearly and unequivocally left to the exclusive authority of the States.'

This, Mr. Chairman, is the doctrine of the Constitution, the doctrine of its framers. It is the doctrine of the Free Soilers. If there

arresting or carrying back his slave. That law secures him against interference on the part of any person to prevent him from arresting and returning his slave. Those who had assisted in framing the constitution, assisted in framing this law. They knew the intention of those who framed the Constitution, and I have no doubt carried that intention into the law of '93.

From that day until the agitation of the annexation of Texas, this doctrine of non-interference was held by southern and northern men. In 1843, this new theory of prostituting the power of this Government in favor

course which I think our northern people will take with regard to it. Let the President hurl his taunts at the freemen of the North. Let him speak of the powers vested in him ; let him use the bayonet, the sword, and the cannon ; let him make himself another Haynau, let him drench our land of freedom with blood ; but he will never make us obey that law. The first cannon that opens its sound upon northern freemen tells the death-knell of this Republic ! I say what before God and man I feel—that the moment your army or navy confronts the freemen of the North, that moment will bring this Republic

Masthead from Voice of the Fugitive, published by Henry Bibb, right

Ironically, soon after settling in her new home, she and Bibb began feuding, and they became bitter enemies.

Mary Shadd's first impression of Windsor was blunt if not generous:

It is, "a mud hole," she said.

In 1851, the year that Henry Bibb launched his newspaper, "Voice of the Fugitive", Shadd started teaching school in a former army barracks that was in such miserable condition that it was abandoned by the army as unfit for use.

Because of the incredible poverty most parents could not afford even a small fee to pay her a nominal salary so Mary Shadd turned to the American Missionary Association (AMA) which agreed to a grant of $125 per year. When Bibb learned of it, he accused her of accepting fees from hard-pressed families while receiving secret support from the association — a white-dominated organization. Normally that might have been little more than a teapot tempest, but by then Bibb and Shadd were already fighting and this new issue put them on a collision course.

Bibb was a founder of the Refugee Home Society, committed to assisting fugitives by buying tracts of land in Essex County and then selling acreage to newly arrived fugitives.

Money was raised by supporters who travelled around speaking and asking for contributions. Shadd scorned such fund-raising as "begging". In a letter to the Missionary Association in 1852 she even accused Bibb of profiteering.

Bibb countered with criticisms of Shadd in his newspaper until, in frustration, she wrote to the association:

"This whole business is really sickening to me. A regular and well executed series of attacks might be resisted by a man of

The Changing Times

The British Methodist Episcopal Church (right) was built in 1856 at what is now University Avenue and Louis Street. It served the congregation until 1963, when a new house of worship was dedicated.

strong physical constitution, but I am not equal to it, I confess ..."

She quit teaching and resurfaced as editor of a black newspaper called "The Provincial Freeman". The first edition was published in Windsor on March 24, 1853.

Realizing that the potential reader base in Windsor-Sandwich was too small, Shadd moved The Freeman to Toronto in 1854, then to Chatham in 1855 but it eventually fell victim to a widespread depression in 1857.

She returned to the U.S. where she accepted a commission as a black recruiting officer during the Civil War.

She later entered law school and became a lawyer at 60.

On June 5, 1893, Mary Ann Shadd "wore out" and died in her daughter's home — cause of death unknown, though the certificate noted that she suffered a tumor of the stomach.

Henry Bibb, born a slave in Kentucky, coveted freedom so fiercely that he attempted to escape six times. The final run was successful and he made his way to Detroit and spent most of the 1840s travelling in Michigan, speaking to abolitionist groups.

In 1850, he moved to Sandwich where he founded the "Voice of the Fugitive" on January 1, 1851.

Most of Bibb's life revolved around support for black fugitives. In addition to helping establish the Home Society, Bibb founded the Canadian Anti-Slavery Society and was named secretary of the Fugitives Union Association. Henry and his wife, Mary, were staunch temperance workers and together they were dubbed the king and queen of the local slave fugitive community.

On October 9, 1853, Bibb's printing office burned ... dealing him a blow from which he never fully recovered. He died on August 1, 1854 — Emancipation Day — convinced that his business had been destroyed by an arsonist in an attack on him personally.

(Sources: 2, 6, 19, 26, 36)

Churches Comforted Blacks In Strange, Cold World

For many of the fugitive slaves who made their way to Canada, the reality of life in their new homeland was not long in coming. While their safe arrival was celebrated as the happy end of one harrowing journey, it also marked the frustrating start of another. With only strange faces to greet them in a bewildering land, these lonely people were in desperate need of kinship and understanding. For that they needed a place to meet; a retreat, where they could gather to mend both body and spirit.

Sandwich Baptist Church — The oldest surviving original black church in Windsor.

While there was nothing to tell them in so many words, the truth was that the established centres (meeting halls, schools, even churches) were white, and mostly out of bounds.

So the freedom-seekers developed their own social order, selected their own ministers, and built their own churches to serve as spiritual and temporal temples.

A number of black congregations were established before 1892 but only four remain.

SANDWICH BAPTIST, the oldest existing original black church, was built in 1851 with hand-made clay bricks fashioned by members who toiled in the evenings after their regular work was done. But even ten years earlier, in 1841, founding members were holding prayer meetings in a log cabin which stood on the site of the present, historic church on Peter Street in the city's west end.

BRITISH METHODIST EPISCOPAL dates to April 13, 1854 when property was deeded to the congregation. Services were held in a small frame structure for two years before the church was completed in 1856. It was demolished in 1963 and the present church was built and dedicated that year.

TANNER AFRICAN METHODIST EPISCOPAL, first called Mercer Street Baptist, was built in 1877. In 1888, Bishop Benjamin E. Tanner bought the building for Windsor's AME congregation. The present church was opened in 1964 after the original was levelled as part of Windsor's downtown redevelopment program.

FIRST BAPTIST was founded by Rev. William Troy, a native of Virginia. In the early days after his arrival in this area Rev. Troy served only Amherstburg, but in 1853 he began travelling to Windsor for prayer meetings. In 1856 he moved to Windsor, organized a black congregation and in 1858 laid the cornerstone for First Baptist Church at McDougall and London Streets (now University). Eventually the congregation decided that a bigger church was needed and on May 24, 1915, the cornerstone was laid for the present church at Mercer and Tuscarora.

(Sources: 4, 19, 26, 54)

Wood fired steam engines like this one first arrived in Windsor in 1854

January 17, 1854 — The Day The Trains Arrived

The first steam locomotive to Windsor will arrive today: Some say it'll be here by one-thirty … others say two o'clock. No matter, two Great Western Railway engines, each pulling six cars, left Niagara Falls early this morning and have already passed London.

This is the moment that people have been talking about for 20 years. A holiday has been declared on both sides of the border.

The mood is sharp with expectation, and well it should be; this single event will open previously unheard of travel and commercial opportunities; it will end the crushing isolation that people suffer at least five months each year.

Ferry boats have been huffing and chuffing back and forth across the Detroit River, bulling their way through thickening pack ice since early morning, disgorging thousands of excited celebrants anxious to find vantage points along the new rail right-of-way.

This is the stuff of history.

There's been a delay; it's well past four o'clock and the crowd is restless. The day started off uncommonly mild but now there's a late afternoon nip in the air as the sun pales and slides towards the horizon. No reason to worry, though; there's more than enough warm cider to go around; besides, hadn't the gangs worked through the night to drop the last rail into place ... ?

They could hear the sound long before they could make out a shape ... off in the distance, to the east ... faintly; the long, low, unmistakable wail of a steam whistle ....

Or were their over-anxious ears playing games again ... ?

Someone shouted: " Over there ... "

The crowd pivoted to the east ... See, down the tracks a quarter mile .... a pack of boys running ... puppets on a string ... arms flailing, legs pumping ...

The crowd grew still, letting the shrill voices carry on the wind: "They're comin' ... they're comin' ... ! ! ! "

The crowd exploded — and from across the river, cannons roared back a mighty salute.

This long-awaited day began at 6:30 when the two wood-burning steam locomotives *London* and *Samson* carrying 600 to 700 passengers left Niagara for Windsor and transfer by ferry to Detroit. By the time they puffed out of Chatham, the number of dignitaries packed into the cars had swelled to almost nine hundred.

Windsor and Detroit, like all stops along the way, were strung and hung with miles of streamers, coloured bunting and hundreds of flags.

One newspaper reporter wrote:

" ... *Most grandly did it sweep along the Canadian shore where the track lies below the bank and in full view of Detroit for nearly a mile ...* "

An hour later the second section arrived:

"*Shouts mingled with the roar of cannon welcomed them and clouds of steam and smoke went up amid the waving banners of the boats dotting the river.*"

Celebrations continued far into the night. Directors and other honoured guests who had been packed into the trains were ferried to Detroit where they were greeted by a military guard-of-honour.

About 2,000 guests moved to the freight sheds of the Michigan

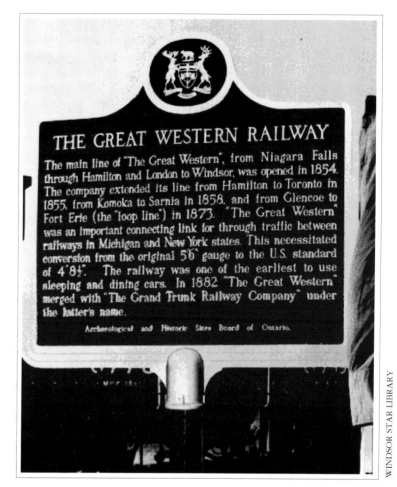

Plaque marks the opening of The Great Western Railway main line from Niagara Falls to Windsor in 1854.

Central in Detroit where they fed on 75 hams, 150 turkeys, 400 chickens and assorted amounts of prairie chickens, quail and legs of mutton — all washed down by an undetermined amount of champagne.

Sixty toasts were drunk to success and prosperity. Such toasts were appropriate because, with the exception of the dawn of the automobile age two decades later, no other event has had such an impact on the social and economic life of the Border Region.

To put it into perspective, let yourself imagine that the only road out of Windsor is a winding, rutted track, little more than a cow path, peppered with boulders and tree stumps. The only land transportation is by horseback, or bone-wrenching wagon. Water transportation is at the whim of the weather. Travel by any means is all but impossible during the winter months. That's what the Border settlers faced until arrival of the trains.

The GWR was conceived in 1834 when a charter was granted under the name of London and Gore Rail Road Co. The company could build a line from London to Burlington Bay and to the navigable waters of the Thames and Lake Huron.

Nothing happened until 1845 when the charter was changed, allowing the company to build a rail line connecting the Niagara and Detroit Rivers. The name was also changed to the Great Western Rail Road Company. In 1853 it was changed again to the Great Western Railway.

In 1855, a year after the Niagara-Windsor line was completed, a GWR subsidiary company connected Hamilton and Toronto. That meant that, with ferry connections between Windsor and Detroit, passengers could, for the first time, travel by rail from the Atlantic Ocean to the Mississippi River.

The GWR was absorbed by the Grand Trunk Railway in 1882 and in 1923 it became part of the Canadian National Railway system.

(Sources: 11, 54)

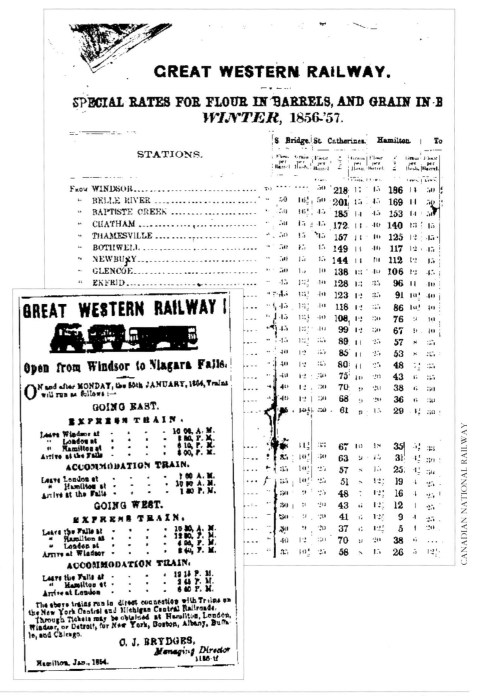

The schedule from the Great Western Railway shown at top right gives the special rates for shipping flour in barrels and grain in bags during the winter of 1856-57.

The Great Western Railway posted its opening schedule for trips from Windsor to Niagara Falls in January, 1854, with the flyer at right.

Horse-powered ferries meant exactly that in the early days along the Detroit River before steam. The first such craft on the Detroit, looking much like this one, was powered by horses walking on a circular table, activating the paddle wheels.

Steam Ferries: Workhorses Of The River

If the decision in 1836 had been to call this riverfront village *"Marine City"* instead of *Windsor* it would have been appropriate and prophetic.

The fact that it was widely known, even then, by such descriptive names as Sandwich Ferry or simply The Ferry, tells us much about the vital role that the Detroit River played in the lives of those who eked out a living along its shores.

Even in those long-ago days ... before the advent of steam ... operating a ferry service was a worthy enterprise, and judging by the remarkable number of vessels that plied the Detroit over the years, it appears that the people enjoyed such a special romance with the river, that the simple act of climbing aboard something to go somewhere else for business or pleasure had become a consuming local pastime.

Nor was there any shortage of imaginative vessels powered by wind, man or animals: there were canoes and rowboats hollowed from huge logs, propelled by paddles, oars and poles; there were catamarans, skiffs, schooners and other sailing craft ranging from common to magnificent; there were horseboats and deep, flat-bottom scows capable of carrying wagons, carriages and cattle.

One of the early operators of a log canoe or rowboat ferry service on this side of the river was Pierre St. Amour who also owned a tavern on the François Baby farm at the foot of what is now Ouellette Avenue. This boat, which could be converted to sail, carried passengers from his tavern to Detroit and back.

Before the advent of steam, horseboats provided a reliable form of locomotion. Captain John Burtis introduced the first horseboat to this area about 1825. Called the *Olive Branch*, it resembled a side-wheeler scow and was powered by two horses walking on a circular table, flush with the deck. The horses remained stationary

Ferries docked at the foot of Ouellette Avenue.

while the table they walked on revolved, activating the shaft which turned the wheel.

The horseboat continued in service until 1833 when Captain Burtis replaced it with the *Argo*, the first steamer to sail the Detroit. There were two vessels by that name. The first, resembling a catamaran, was composed of two immense, hollowed whitewood logs topped by a makeshift deck and powered by a four-horsepower engine. The original *Argo* was replaced by another boasting a more conventional single hull.

Records indicate that between 1833 and 1892, at least 30 steamships of various kinds were launched and worked the river and connecting lakes. They included freighters, passenger ferries, car ferries and cattle boats. Some served for decades while others

sank, were destroyed by fire, decommissioned or sold for service elsewhere. One of the oldest, the *Lansdowne*, built in 1884, was converted in 1983 to a floating restaurant on the Detroit riverfront.

These great steamships provided comfortable and relatively swift transportation from Windsor and Detroit to such places as Toledo, Amherstburg, Chatham, Port Huron, Sarnia and Buffalo.

An event of intense interest in 1867 was the construction of the *Great Western*, the first ferry to haul rail cars across the river. She was built of iron in Scotland and shipped here in sections for assembly in Henry Jenkin's Walkerville shipyard. The launching attracted particular attention because many believed that an iron ship of that size would never float.

(Sources: 20, 54)

The Argo 2 *(right)was launched in 1848 to replace its namesake, Argo 1, built in 1830. Argo 1 was an awkward, twin-hulled craft.*

The powerful, steam driven car ferry Lansdowne *(left) was built in 1884 and served until 1983 when it was converted to a floating restaurant in Detroit.*

It wasn't until 1890, 36 years after the arrival of the Great Western Railway, that the Canadian Pacific Railway decided to carve its own niche in this corner of the province. At that time, Sir William Van Horne, president of the CPR, knowing that important salt deposits were being mined on the other side of the river, gambled that they were present in Windsor as well. Tests on riverfront property between Crawford and Caron avenues proved him right. Having the ability to carry passengers west and return east with cargoes of salt proved a boon to the CPR. Canadian Salt Company buildings are just to the left of the CPR tower and passenger station.

Birth Of A City

Through the fall of 1865 and spring of 1866, the air was filled with rumours of possible raids by Fenians, bands of Irish agitators seeking to strike a blow at Britain. Twelve companies of infantry arrived to help defend the border region — against attacks which never came. Some of the defending troops were quartered in the original Assumption College building at right. Although one account says the men on the roof were on lookout alert for possible advancing Fenian raiders, other speculation suggests it is more likely they were simply hamming it up for a passing photographer.

When The Jesuits Came, A College Was Born

The history pages of Assumption College are filled with the names of dozens of people who played roles, large and small, in its founding — but no name looms as large as that of Rev. Pierre Point, the Jesuit priest who stands as its chief architect, and driving force. Without Father Point's vision and stubborn determination, it is probable that the college (forerunner of The University of Windsor) would not have been built.

Father Point, born (1802) and educated in France, was ordained in 1826, joined the Society of Jesus in 1839, emigrated to Quebec in 1843 and was posted to Assumption parish. Although he was slight in stature and outwardly mild-mannered he had enormous en-

ergy, was meticulous, tough-minded and not intimidated by people or events.

It was on the last day of 1854, while writing his year-end report to his superior in Fordham, New York, that Father Point sketched his ideas for a new Jesuit college to be built on the boundary between Windsor and Sandwich in this remote corner of Essex County in Canada West.

It was an idea whose time had come. There was much talk that Sandwich would become a town within the next three or four years; plans were afoot to build a new courthouse in the new year; arrival of the Great Western Railroad in Windsor had thrown

Drawing from "Historic Sandwich Town" shows Assumption University, which is the Catholic College within the University of Windsor.

CITY OF WINDSOR (WACAC) / ARTIST BYRON LEE

open the doors of opportunity; the population was climbing steadily.

Earlier in the year the priest had met with parish leaders and they shared his vision. The college would rise between the orchard and the cemetery; it would be 90 feet long, 50 feet wide and three stories high and it would accommodate up to 60 day students.

When approval from his superior arrived, Father Point wasted no time. Construction began in May 1855 and the school opened on February 10, 1857 with 26 boarders and 60 day students. From the beginning, Assumption College was many things. It was the first secondary school for young men in Southern Ontario; it was

the common school of Sandwich, managed by Theodule Girardot and his family, without whose efforts it might not have survived; it was a classical college, preparing boys for either the priesthood or for such professions as law and medicine — it was the only school of its kind between Notre Dame in Indiana and St. Michael's in Toronto.

Ironically, completion of the college was a bitter-sweet climax to many long, tiring months of planning and hard work. Instead of contributing to a foundation of harmony and goodwill, it triggered years of intra-church animosity, hostility and petty turf wars among priests, bishops, religious orders and the lay community.

Before long, the Jesuits found themselves the victims of their own success in an interesting and convoluted way. On the one hand the college had grown too big, too fast and the Society didn't have enough priests to run both it and the parish; on the other hand the college was too small to fit into the Jesuits' grand scheme of things. After some discussion, the superiors decided to consolidate their resources in New York and in December 1859, the Assumption Jesuits were recalled and reassigned to other duties.

For years after the official opening, operation of the college was bedevilled by a variety of bad decisions. Following the departure of the Jesuits from Sandwich, the college was managed in turn by a Basilian, several diocesan priests and the German-speaking Benedictines from Pennsylvania. The turn-around didn't begin until 1870 when responsibility was returned to the Basilians — this time under the leadership of Father Dennis O'Connor who served for 20 years before becoming Bishop of London and Archbishop of Toronto.

Father Point's Assumption College was incorporated in 1858 and additions were made in 1875, 1886 and 1907. An L-shaped length of the foundation of the original college is all that remains and it has been preserved as a landmark. Today, Assumption University is the Catholic College in the University of Windsor.

Father Point, who returned to Montreal, died there at the College Sainte-Marie in September, 1896 at the age of 94.

(Sources: 29, 37, 44, 54)

The Foundation House which later grew into St. Mary's Academy was opened in 1864 as the "Select School for Girls". It was located on the east side of Goyeau Street, south of Park Street.

St. Mary's: An Academy Built On Faith

They weren't supposed to have arrived so soon; the townspeople weren't ready for the newcomers; there should have been more time to make proper arrangements! But the telegraph message was quite specific:

"Sisters Marie Jean Baptiste, Marie Alphonse, Marie Mathilde and Marie Thomas will arrive at the Windsor station on October 20, 1864 at 8 a.m."

There was a touch of autumn in the air as the Great Western puffed into town carrying, among others, the four young women, Sisters of the Holy Names of Jesus and Mary. They would become the founders of St. Mary's Academy.

Although they didn't know a soul and had only four dollars among them, on November 28, scarcely a month after their arrival, they moved into what was to become the Foundation House, a two-storey brick building at Goyeau and London (now University) Streets. This "Select School for Girls" opened with seven day-students and two boarders. The fact that others were turned away

Immediately after the Foundation House was opened, plans were made to build a finer structure (above) near St. Alphonsus Church. For years, the Academy was the most attractive building in the city. Additions were made in 1870, 1884 and 1904, when it appeared as shown at right.

for lack of space; indicated there was a need, so plans were laid for a larger, finer building near St. Alphonsus Church. Work began in October, 1865 and the sisters took possession of the first St. Mary's Academy in November 1867.

For years the Academy, easily the most impressive building in town, was affectionately known as "Windsor Castle".

In 1927 plans were announced for construction of the Detroit-Windsor tunnel, and the Canadian terminal would be on the site then occupied by the Academy. Negotiations were completed for a $1,000,000 purchase price and construction of the new Academy on a 23-acre site was completed in September 1929.

Beautiful as the building was, in the 1970s a decision was made to sell the property to a private developer. The Academy was demolished in May 1977, making way for St. Mary's Gate, a housing development in South Windsor.

(Sources: 40, 42, 54)

Members of a hook-and-ladder brigade (about 1890) strike a classic 19th Century pose for the photographer. St. Mary's Academy is visible through the trees.

Flames: The Ultimate Scourge Of The 19th Century

Fire, the scourge of settlers living in unprotected, tinder-dry shoebox homes came close to turning Windsor into an ash pile on at least two occasions in the mid 1800s. The worst, known generally, if not fondly, as "The Great Windsor Fire" started in the early hours of October 12, 1871. Speculation is that an overheated tailor's iron might have been the culprit. Before the fire was contained, many buildings in a three-block area were either destroyed or severely damaged.

While the individual losses were heavy, in the end there were benefits:

- Destruction of downtown buildings allowed the widening of Ouellette Avenue to 75 feet from 50;
- Many wooden buildings were replaced with brick;
- Construction created jobs;
- The waterworks system — a fleet of water carts designed for door-to-door delivery — was replaced with a pipeline.

In an earlier fire, on April 16, 1849, the entire village of 300 people came close to being wiped out when sparks from the wood-burning steamer *Hastings* ignited a pile of dry cedar posts on François Baby's wharf near the foot of Ferry Street. The flames quickly spread to James Dougall's store, Baby's customs house, the Ferry Saloon, the Prince Albert Hotel and a number of other homes and shops.

As the bucket brigade struggled against impossible odds, Baby brought a Detroit Fire Department company and pumper across on his own ferry, the *Alliance*. At the same time the captain of another ferry was persuaded to cross the choppy river with additional men and equipment.

Baby was grateful to the Detroit Fire Department and raised enough money at a public meeting to present the Detroit firemen with a silver speaking trumpet which is now preserved in the Detroit Historical Museum.

(Sources: 11, 34, 35, 54)

*Photographer captured crowd scene on Sandwich Street the morning after
the fire levelled much of Windsor's business core in 1871. This view is looking
west from Ouellette Avenue.*

New buildings on Sandwich Street, many of them brick, replaced those destroyed by 1871 fire. Ouellette Avenue was also widened during the reconstruction process. This view is looking east from Church Street.

The Changing Times

Construction of Hotel Dieu hospital was started on October 10, 1888 and completed at a cost of $38,543. This building was demolished in 1963.

Rev. J. T. Wagner, born in Germany in 1837, was Dean of Essex and served as pastor of St. Alphonsus parish for 32 years. He took ill in the late 1890s and returned to Germany, where he died on August 26, 1897.

Mother Paquet, first Superior of Hotel Dieu, was born in Joliette, Quebec on October 15, 1845. She entered the Order of the Religious Hospitallers of St. Joseph, also known as the Hotel Dieu Sisters, at the age of 23. Mother Paquet returned to Montreal in 1904 and died in 1917.

Hotel Dieu: The Impossible Dream

It probably would have happened sooner or later, perhaps at a different time, in a different way, but the founding of Hotel Dieu Hospital is closely linked with a Catholic priest's desire to help black children — and a religious order's vow to minister to the sick.

The nuns were the Religious Hospitallers of St. Joseph, the priest was Rev. J. T. Wagner, better known as Dean Wagner.

Dean Wagner had long been bothered by the plight of young blacks, the destitute children of the fugitives who had fled the slave states years before. Many were now homeless, uneducated and barred from white schools. He believed that an orphanage and day-school were desperately needed.

In the fall of 1887, Dean Wagner, the St. Alphonsus parish priest, launched a letter campaign asking for donations — even a dime — to help build the orphanage. One letter was received by Mother Bonneau, Montreal Superior of the Religious Hospitallers of St. Joseph. She sent $2.50 and suggested that the Order might be interested in building a hospital in Windsor, and asked Dean Wagner for his response.

Dean Wagner thanked her and, while acknowledging that a hospital was needed, helping the black children remained his goal. He also knew that the Sisters of St. Joseph had a reputation for getting things done and he saw an opportunity to achieve both: he suggested to Mother Bonneau that they work together to build the hospital *and* a black orphanage and day school. Although Mother Bonneau was cool to the suggestion, Dean Wagner persisted.

Along the way he also confessed that instead of having $10,000 put aside as he had originally told her, he had less than $8,000 — far short of the $40,000 needed to build the hospital, let alone an orphanage. Furthermore, he would not be able to provide the customary financial support to the nuns themselves. He said that if they decided to join him, they should bring along $5,000 to cover living expenses which he would consider as an interest-free loan, without any repayment guarantee from him.

How would they raise the rest of the money? Through the sale of used stamps to collectors, annual bazaars, and blind faith in Providence. It was a most unusual arrangement for the hospitallers to consider, but after protracted negotiations and many prayers they agreed. A site-selection committee arrived and chose six lots at Ouellette Avenue and Erie Street, at a cost of $3,300.

On Friday September 14, 1888 five nuns, including Sister Josephine Paquet, the founding superior, arrived to launch the hospital, orphanage and day-school projects. They lived for the first 18 months in makeshift quarters in St. Alphonsus parish hall. Hospital tenders were called and the contract for the stone and brickwork was given to Hypolite Reaume; the carpenter and joiner work went to Henry Walker. Construction began on Wednesday, October 10, 1888.

The cornerstone was laid on November 29; the hospital was dedicated in October, 1889 and opened in February, 1890. The first horse-drawn ambulance was bought for $450 in 1891. Prior to that, if an ambulance was needed it was brought from Detroit by boat.

Dean Wagner's interest in educating the black children began in 1887 when he formed a local society to work with him in establishing the Catholic Coloured School under the direction of the Holy Name Sisters. It was dogged by poor attendance and was closed after only 18 months.

Dean Wagner was disappointed but he persisted and his agreement with the Sisters of St. Joseph led to the building of a wood-frame orphanage and day school adjacent to the hospital. It opened on May 30, 1890. By 1893, 25 live-in orphans had been admitted and the day student enrolment peaked at 55. Unfortunately, attendance fell off and despite their best efforts, the nuns couldn't entice more than 10 or 15 students to attend at any one time. In March they called it quits and the building was donated to the Catholic School Board.

(Sources: Hotel Dieu Archives, 53, 54)

Queen's Birthday
MAY 24, 1892.

CITY
· OF ·
WINDSOR

INAUGURATION.

Part Four:

Upstream — Downstream

From Walkerville To Sandwich

Distiller, industrialist, Hiram Walker died at 83.

His name was Hiram Walker; he was a New England clerk-turned-Detroit-grocer-turned-Canadian-landowner-miller and distiller: He was a visionary . . . an entrepreneur . . . an industrialist . . . a philanthropist.

He built a town called Walkerville.

This is the story of the town and its founder — the two are inseparable.

Hiram Walker was born in Massachusetts, perhaps somewhat prophetically, on the Fourth of July — in 1816. By all accounts he was a man with a contradictory personal makeup. On the one hand he was described as pensive and thoughtful; on the other, he had a restless soul with an entrepreneurial spirit. He took pride in pinching pennies, but would gamble thousands on a variety of challenges from making vinegar, to cattle raising, to flour milling, and, of course, making whisky.

One aspect about which there is little debate is that he was a relentless, driven worker. He had enormous energy and strove constantly to keep his body up to "concert pitch."

At 20 he left home for Boston, working as a clerk before joining thousands of easterners trekking to the Midwest. Walker's destination was Detroit where he became involved in a series of business ventures, none of which was particularly successful, until he opened a wholesale and retail grocery store on Atwater Street. In the 1850s, Detroit grocery stores were allowed to sell liquor, and Hiram Walker, though a non-drinker, recognizing the profit opportunities of producing his own spirits, began experimenting with a process of recovering alcohol from wine.

By 1854 he produced his first barrel of hard liquor — an event which set him on the road to modest fame and considerable fortune.

Rare photo of "The Cottage", the Walkerville home that Hiram Walker lived in for five years. It was adjacent to the company head office on Riverside Drive.

Three years later, at the age of 41, his personal wealth standing at a tidy $40,000, his mind was fired with thoughts of establishing a flour mill and distillery on the Canadian side of the Detroit River.

The timing was perfect: he would build a steam-driven flour mill where none existed; there was little serious distillery competition on this side of the river; arrival of the Great Western Railway three years earlier opened enormous new trade opportunities. In addition, the increasing agitation of prohibitionists in his own country made him nervous about the future of the liquor industry there.

He bought almost 500 acres of land a few miles upstream from Windsor and built The Windsor Distillery and Flouring Mill.

Within the year his distillery met expectations and his steam-powered grain mill outproduced the plodding wind-driven mills that dotted the area.

In the beginning the community was known as *Walker's Town* and while it is uncertain when *"Walkerville"* gained general usage, records show that government recognition came in 1869 with the establishment of a post office.

Launching the mill and distillery was only a start. An obvious distillery byproduct is mash which, depending on your viewpoint, is either bothersome waste or valuable livestock feed. Hiram Walker decided on the latter which led him into the livestock business. He built pens to house 500 hogs adjacent to the distillery

Walkerville Boat Club was the centre of social life in the 1880s.

but an outbreak of cholera forced him out of hogs and into cattle. In 1882 fire swept the Walkerville waterfront and wiped out the cattle barns. New brick sheds were built near Tecumseh and Walker Roads and swill from the distillery fattened his livestock as well as his bank account.

A byproduct of hundreds of cattle is tons of manure which was used to fertilize acres of tobacco, hops, wheat, oats and barley. The grain was used in his distillery to make whisky which was popular in the U.S. One brand called "Club" was in such demand that protectionist legislation was introduced in the U.S. requiring foreign distillers to show the country of origin on the labels. Although the strategy was intended to discourage drinkers from supporting "foreign" spirits, it backfired when Walker added the name "Canadian" to "Club" and loyalty spread internationally.

Walker continued to improve his village; fine homes on tree-lined streets were served by schools, water, street lights as well as fire and police protection. He even built a church in 1870. Since most of the villagers professed to be Methodists, Walker invited that denomination to serve the congregation. The first preacher was a student minister who avoided speaking about the evils of drink. Two years later he was replaced by an ordained minister who made the mistake of railing against demon rum — and he was invited to take his sacred messages elsewhere. The church remained closed until 1874 when it was turned over to the Anglican Synod and renamed St. Mary's in honour of Walker's late wife, Mary Abigail.

Two views of the Walkerville Ferry Dock. Above: Approaching aboard ferry on the Detroit River. Right: The view from Walkerville.

Sandwich Street in Walkerville, looking east from Devonshire Road. The Hiram Walker "flat iron" building is in the right foreground.

Hiram Walker maintained active businesses in Detroit as well and, in his own view, wasted too much time travelling by ferry from one side to the other, so in 1880 he established his own ferry service with a terminal in Walkerville. Although his heart was in Detroit, he lived from 1859 to 1864 in Walkerville, in a remodelled house known as The Cottage. He returned to Detroit and remained there until his death on Thursday, January 12, 1899 at the age of 83.

Ronald Hoskins, a University of Windsor History professor and authority on Walkerville, notes that Walkerville remained a relatively small community well into the 1880s. By the 1890s other industries had moved into the area including the drug firm of Parke Davis, Globe Furniture Company, Walkerville Malleable Iron Company, the Ontario Basket Company and Milner-Walker Wagon Works, which was the forerunner of the Ford Motor Company of Canada.

Times were changing and in January, 1890 a petition was submitted to the provincial legislature supporting Walkerville's incorporation as a town. Prominent among the 208 names on the petition were those of the Walker family. The change in status would achieve several goals. First, it would release the family from the financial burden of maintaining police and fire departments, but more important, in Hoskins' view, was the fear of annexation by Windsor. While incorporation as a town wouldn't hold Windsor's expansionists back forever, it would delay the inevitable.

Incorporation became official on April 7, 1890 — two years before Windsor became a city. Hiram A. Walker, nephew of the founder, became the first mayor. The first council meeting was held on May 12, 1890 and the first order of business was to declare July 4 — the founder's birthday — a public holiday.

(Sources: 7, 21, 22, 54)

An 1833 sketch of the waterfront in Sandwich shows the Jacques Baby House (enlarged to show detail at right).

MINISTRY OF CULTURE AND COMMUNICATIONS

Sandwich Town: One Of Ontario's Oldest Historic Settlements

It's doubtful that there exists in Ontario, another square mile that has been witness to as much history-in-the-making as the one that gave birth to the Town of Sandwich. Even today, the very mention of the name "Sandwich" evokes powerful images of battles won and lost; of unsought and unsung heroism; of the pure, rawhide-toughness needed to survive in those early frontier days .

In its time, Sandwich has been home or host to some of the most renowned military and political figures in the land including Major General Isaac Brock; Tecumseh, the battle-tested Shawnee Indian chief; the indomitable Col. John Prince; Henry Bibb the embattled fugitive slave turned newspaper publisher; Alexander Mackenzie, stonemason, politician and second prime minister of Canada; Jacques (James) Baby, Inspector General of Upper Canada and Speaker of the Legislative Council ...

The list goes on, but see for yourself. Make yourself comfortable in the shade of that large chestnut tree in what was commonly known as Bedford Square. Now, suspend disbelief and watch the passing parade.

From here you will see the coming of the Jesuit missionaries and watch them sow the seeds for what will become the first Roman Catholic parish in Upper Canada; they'll be followed soon by the first permanent European settlers in what is now Ontario.

You'll see the beginning of Alexander Duff's fur trading post — one of the earliest in the Border Region.

Mason-Girardot Manor (circa 1875) at 3203 Peter Street (right) has been restored and is a popular dining place.

McGregor-Cowan house (circa 1806) at 3118 Sandwich Street (left), now the home of Zoli Antiques, was home of the Canadian Emigrant, Essex County's first newspaper in the 1830s.

Dominion House (circa 1875), now at 3140 Sandwich Street, was located across the street until it burned in 1879. It was rebuilt on the north side of Sandwich Street, where it stands today. Known warmly as "The DH", it is a popular meeting and eating place.

You'll hear shots fired and see men fall in the opening salvos of the War of 1812.

You'll see a contingent of General William Hull's men in full retreat after being ambushed by the British.

Cross the street to the Anglican cemetery and you'll see the funeral of Dr. John James Hume, killed by a rag-tag marauding band of so-called "patriots". Five were later executed by Col. Prince who denounced them as pirates, not patriots.

You will see excited preparations to thwart an attack by gangs of anti-British Irish-Americans known as the Fenians, if ever a raid comes — which it doesn't.

Your sensitivities will be shattered as you witness the last two public hangings at Sandwich jail. You'll be shocked even more to learn that the law says the bodies are to be hung in public view in an iron corset known as a "gibbet iron".

You will see proud ceremonies taking place around the site of the new courthouse as dignitaries gather to lay a cornerstone, engraved with the date, 1855. In the crowd you'll notice a mild-mannered man who walks with a slight limp. His name is Alexander Mackenzie. He will build this fine new structure and one day soon after he will become Canada's second prime minister.

No wonder this square mile of land which became the centre of law and government for the entire Western District — what we know as Essex, Kent and Lambton Counties — is reputed to be one of the most historic square miles in Upper Canada!

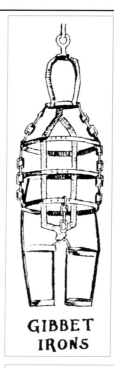

GIBBET IRONS

The gibbet irons, left, were a posthumous punishment for the most serious offenders. After death by hanging, the corpse was strapped into the irons and hung from a pole on public display, below, to deter any who might be tempted to follow in the offender's footsteps.

Murderer or Horse Thief Beware!

If you were a convicted murderer or horse thief early in the 19th Century, you would likely end your days at the end of a rope — after which your body, encased in a steel corset called a gibbet iron, would be hung from a pole in public "until the flesh rotted from the bones."

This practice, called gibbeting, was demanded by the law and it wasn't a pretty sight but the idea was to discourage dastardly deeds by exposing criminals to public scorn.

Although it isn't known when the practice ended, records show that sometime before 1830, two young men from Chatham were the last to be gibbetted in Sandwich. Their steel-strapped bodies were hung from poles on the brow of the hill on Russell Street where they were left twisting in the wind until villagers complained about the offensive sight and smell. One night the bodies disappeared and no questions were asked. In 1889, men working at a gravel pit, uncovered a skeleton and the iron frame of a gibbet which is now in the Hiram Walker Historical Museum collection.

Public executions, which attracted people like bears to honey were carried out at the Sandwich Jail until 1862. The last person to have the distinction of being hanged publicly was a 38-year-old man by the name of George Williams, who killed his wife with an axe and then cut his own throat. Ironically, his bleeding body was discovered in time for doctors to make him well enough to be hanged in public on a bitterly cold Friday, January 3, 1862.

(Sources: 35, 54)

Crowds gather at the Western Hotel and the old courthouse building (now Mackenzie Hall) in Bedford Square, focal point of public activities in Sandwich. At the time this photo was taken, the Border Region was on alert against possible raids by anti-British Fenians living in the U.S. The Fenians wanted an end to British rule in Ireland. Although attacks occurred in other areas, none took place here. One unconfirmed explanation for this scene is that the townspeople gathered in response to one of a number of false alarms that a Fenian raid was imminent.

A Prime Minister's Historic Legacy

From an architectural standpoint, the solid, two-storey, sandy-coloured limestone building in the heart of Old Sandwich won't leave you breathless, but it is one of the most historically important buildings in town.

Its uniqueness lies in the fact that it was built in 1855-56 as a county courthouse and jail by Alexander Mackenzie — the man who would become Canada's second prime minister: It is the only such building existing in Canada.

Today it is known as Mackenzie Hall in honour of the Scottish-born stonemason-prime minister whose company, Mackenzie Builders, won the contract to build it in 1855. It cost about $8,000 to build — and close to $3,000,000 to rehabilitate 130 years later.

When it opened in December, 1856, it was the fourth courthouse on the site in Bedford Square, (now Brock and Sandwich Streets). The first, a crude blockhouse, was rafted down from Chatham in 1797; a second structure was built in 1799, and a third was built about 1818-1820. The second and third were burned. By 1959, after serving for more than a century as the home of law and

Carving above the doorway at Mackenzie Hall depicts the original seal of Essex County.

government for the Western District of Upper Canada it was evident that it was no longer able to meet contemporary needs and the last tenant moved out by 1975. Soon after it was abandoned and declared "surplus" by the provincial government, the official mood shifted towards reducing it to a parking lot: enter a group of preservationists, led by Evelyn McLean, a student of historic architecture with a special interest in Windsor's timeless west end.

McLean, a member of the Essex County Historical Society convinced a group of 15 people that the building was worth saving. They surfaced publicly as Friends of the Court and launched a campaign that lasted seven years. The city capitulated and bought the property from the province — for $1 plus $200 in legal costs.

Mackenzie Hall now serves as an important cultural and entertainment centre; the massive entranceway has been named the McLean Room, in honour of the woman who wouldn't let her dream fade.

(Sources: 35, 44, 54)

Mackenzie Hall Cornerstone

Soldier, Sheriff Ordained As St. John's First Pastor

It's not as though Richard Pollard, soldier, lawyer, sheriff and judge didn't have enough to do during the week that he had to spend his Sundays as an Anglican lay preacher in Sandwich, years before there was either a congregation or a church building.

But he did devote the Lord's Day to leading prayer services and preaching the Gospel, and that devotion led to his ordination, first as a deacon then as a priest — and the creation of the earliest Anglican parish in Ontario, west of Niagara. Those events gave him a place in history as the founding father of the dioceses of Huron and Michigan, as well as recognition as one of the community pillars in this rough-and-tumble frontier community in the early 1800s. Pollard moved to Sandwich from Detroit in the late 1790s and was 52 years old when he was ordained a priest in 1804.

As there was no Anglican clergyman here, each Sunday, beginning as early as 1796, Sheriff Pollard invited people to services in a building that served as government offices. There he read the Church of England services and printed sermons. Such an informal arrangement might have been sufficient in a community more genteel than Sandwich. However, Peter Russell, administrator of the province, felt that more was needed and in a letter to Bishop Jacob Mountain of Quebec in February 1798, said:

". . . Yet it is at the same time my wish that no time should be lost in placing a discreet good Clergyman at Sandwich and giving him a Church there; because its Vicinage to a Military Frontier of the United States whose soldiers are daily deserting to this Side, exposes it to a most dangerous Contagion; which if not early opposed by the improved Morals of its Inhabitants may spread wide and be ultimately productive of every Evil that can be apprehended from a total disregard to all the Duties we owe to God and Man. The Necessity of such an antidote is moreover strongly impressed on my mind by a letter which I have just received from the Chairman of the Bench for the Western District, where he implores my immediate assistance towards

CITY OF WINDSOR (WACAC) / ARTIST BYRON LEE

Pen and ink sketch from "Historic Sandwich Town" shows St. John's Anglican Church as it is today.

This architect's drawing, dated May 28, 1821, was for a proposed steeple for St. John's Anglican Church. It is believed that this, the second church, opened in 1820 and looked much like the first, which burned in 1813. The steeple was never built.

Rev. Richard Pollard's gravestone in St. John's Church cemetery.

rebuilding their Jail which has been lately burnt — as they have no proper place to confine the Multitudes of American Deserters who are daily committed by the Magistrates for every Crime that can blacken a New Year Kalendar."

That was more easily said than done. There were few ministers in England who were anxious to come to such a vast, problem-ridden diocese. For that reason, the bishop sought mature men with some liberal education, and Sheriff Pollard was well suited. Sandwich was the base from which he served Fort Malden, Colchester, Chatham and Detroit — no mean task considering that a round-trip covered at least 240 miles. Except for a period during the War of 1812 when he was taken prisoner, his ministry ran from 1802 until his death in 1824 at the age of 72.

The first church building, a square, log structure built on the present site in 1803, stood until 1813 when it burned. While proof is inconclusive, a popular account is that it was torched by General William Harrison's Kentucky Rifles in either late September or early October. The second church was opened on June 11, 1820 and the third (present) church, on June 23, 1873. The basement and the base of the steeple from the second church were incorporated in the third.

(Sources: 47, 54)

They Billed It As "The Most Valuable Water In The World"

If you stand at the northern edge of the gravel shoulder roughly where Sandwich and John Streets meet, and give your imagination free rein, you might pick out the traces of a shallow, north-south cleavage in the earth — all that remains of what was once one of the most popular natural tourist attractions this side of Niagara Falls. In its heyday it was a wide, peaceful, tree-lined lagoon running from the river's edge to a mineral springs bath and spa at its head. It was a magnet for thousands of visitors who came seeking a quiet weekend retreat or because they believed the warm mineral waters gushing from the earth could give relief from illnesses ranging from rheumatism to liver complications.

Development of this health spa was accidental and is one of the lesser known but more interesting aspects of life in late-19th Century Sandwich. In 1866, when the search for oil was firing imaginations, a group of investors believed petroleum existed in Sandwich. A fund-raising meeting held at the Western Hotel brought in $10,000, which was used to form the Sandwich Petroleum Oil Company.

Drilling equipment was installed and, although they didn't raise a pint of oil, at 900 feet they hit a rich, sulphurous mineral spring which turned out to be the next best thing.

Sightseers poured in and before townspeople realized what was happening, they were in the midst of a tourist boom. The oil company built a bath house and John Gauthier, who owned the property, built the Mineral Springs Hotel (later Lagoon Park Hotel). Not surprisingly, a hired analyst pronounced it "the most valuable water in the world". They called it Sandwich Mineral Springs.

A canal was dug from the Detroit River; trees were planted along the banks and a boat livery opened, creating a popular weekend destination for family outings; boat fare from Detroit was 25 cents return; hack operators charged 10 cents – one way from the Windsor Ferry landing. Writers have since claimed that 20,000 to 25,000 visitors would arrive on a Sunday — a figure that seems exaggerated.

Sandwich Mineral Springs drew large crowds until about 1889 when the springs lost their allure and the site was closed in 1891. The hotel and bath house were taken down and the lagoon silted in.

The park, first called Sandwich Mineral Springs was renamed Manhattan Park and later, Lagoon Park.

(Sources: 54)

Young people take a relaxing canoe ride on the man-made mineral springs at Lagoon Park close to where Sandwich and John Streets meet.

Queen's Birthday
MAY 24, 1892.

CITY
· OF ·
WINDSOR
INAUGURATION.

Part Five:

An Historic
Photo Album

Sandwich Street in downtown Windsor was a bustling place when this photo was taken around the turn of the century. The scene is looking east on Sandwich from Ferry Street. The White Building is the second structure from the right. The tower at the top left corner is the Opera House.

Photo Album

The International Hotel was built at the southwest corner of Ouellette Avenue, fronting on Sandwich Street, following the fire of 1871.

Windsor High School, a four-room structure, was located near the southeast corner of Goyeau and Park streets from 1877 to 1895. It was renamed Windsor Collegiate Institute and was the forerunner of Patterson Collegiate.

1863 photo, looking east along unpaved Sandwich Street in Windsor, is one of the earliest known to exist. Travel by stage coach between Windsor and Sandwich was still common.

In the lower centre portion of the photo, stage operator Joseph Ouellette appears to be collecting his fare from arriving passengers. The one-way fare between the two communities was 12 cents. The only route available was along the riverbank. The road was maintained by the Sandwich and Windsor Gravel Road Company. Revenue was collected at a toll gate established mid-way between the two communities. Eventually, a horse-drawn street railway line made stage travel obsolete. Among the names that appear on the buildings are Ashley and Gilkes, Ouellette and Langlois, and Cameron and Thorburn.
(Source: 35)

Birth Of A City

COVER PHOTO: Once Windsor achieved full City status, growth and improved prosperity followed. One of the barometers of community progress was development of the electric street car system. By 1893 service was available on Sandwich Street, London Street (now University Avenue) and Ouellette Avenue, south to what is now Jackson Park. This scene is looking north on Ouellette, toward Detroit. The smokestack in the distance is that of a steamship at the Ferry Landing. The intersecting street is Pitt. The building on the immediate left is the Post Office. Across the street, to the north, is the Laing Building, which stands today.

Although Hiram Walker is known for the distillery he built in 1857-58, his active business interests included everything from flour milling to livestock to newspapers — and railroading. On December 26, 1888, he opened the Lake Erie, Essex and Detroit River Railroad — better known as "Hiram Walker's Railroad" (right). The passenger and freight line eventually ran 126 miles from Walkerville to St. Thomas.

Ferry Landing. **Windsor,** Canada.

Use of postcards, to send greetings to friends and relatives in distant cities or foreign countries, gained wide popularity at the turn of the century. Because they were highly treasured and saved by those receiving them, they have since become one of our most important sources of information to show us how people lived in those earlier days. Thousands of postcards like this one (left) still exist in private collections and give us an excellent perspective on the importance of the Windsor Ferry Landing at the foot of Ouellette Avenue.

SALTMARCHE, TORONTO

This untitled painting [River Scene, Sunset, Windsor, Ontario] by Frederick Arthur Verner in 1891, offers a panoramic view looking west along Sandwich Street. The conical tower was part of the Canadian Pacific Railway station, opened in 1890. Verner produced many works of this area while visiting his parents, who lived in Sandwich. His father was mayor for two terms. The painting, a gift of the Women's Committee of the Art Gallery of Windsor, is in the Gallery's permanent collection.

Photo Album

It's difficult to overstate the importance of Windsor-Detroit ferry service on the economy of the Border Region in the 19th Century. At times, the river was churned to a froth by the endless chain of passenger, freight and rail ships. For that reason, the ferry landing at the foot of Ouellette Avenue was probably the most important international crossing point in the province. Nor was there any commonality of design or size. They were as small as the passenger ferry Essex (preceding page) or as large as the Great Western (right). The Great Western, a car ferry and the first iron ship to be built in the area, began service on January 1, 1867.

As Detroit and Windsor continued to grow through the 1890s, river traffic increased with links to virtually every port on the Upper Great Lakes. With that came larger, more luxurious steamers, including the Promise (left). It was built in Detroit in 1892. In later years, the Promise along with a sister ship, the Pleasure, maintained a 10-minute service between Windsor and Detroit.

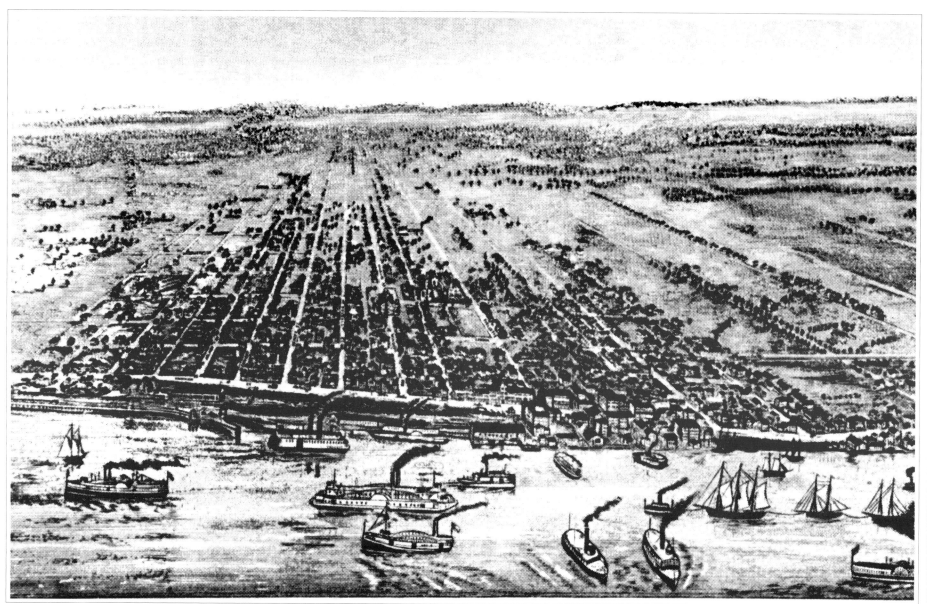

Detailed 1878 "bird's eye view" provides an important look at marine activity on the Detroit River and as well as an opportunity to see how well Windsor had developed. When the early French families settled in the area, they clustered on the river and established long, narrow "strip farms" fronting on the water. That plan provided more people with direct access to the water — the community's "main street".

HIRAM WALKER HISTORICAL MUSEUM

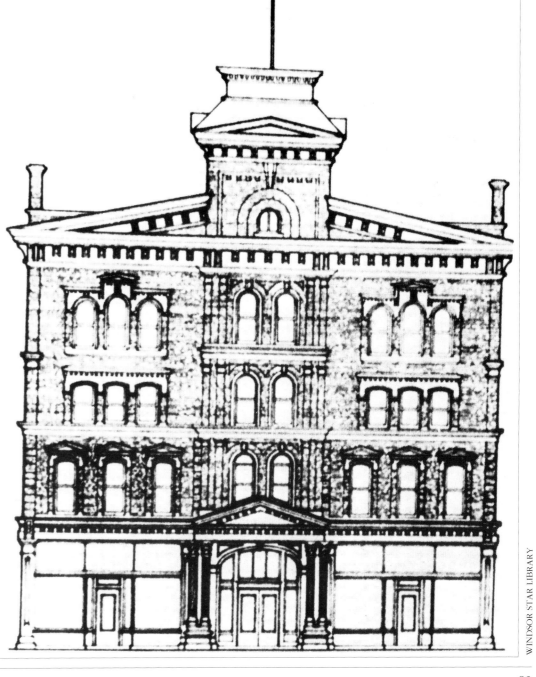

There isn't so much as a foundation stone left to remind us that the Windsor Opera House (right), once stood on Sandwich Street just east of Ouellette Avenue. The 800-seat theatre was opened in 1882 with a performance of something called "Ten Nights in a Bar Room." The enterprise was not successful and its owner, John W. Davis, then mayor of Windsor, rang down the curtain in December, 1901. The building was levelled in November, 1978.

The arrival of wood-burning steam engines in 1854 opened new vistas for those living in virtual isolation in this far corner of the Western District. The early GWR locomotive (preceding page) was one of the earliest to serve the Windsor area. Heavy mesh screens covering the wide smoke stack prevented hot embers from breaking loose to ignite the countryside. Not all railway lines operated with the same gauge track and it was necessary to have a "third rail" as shown in the photo above of the GWR yards in Windsor.

High elevation view looking west between Pitt and Sandwich streets, provides an excellent perspective of the "downtown" area.

Birth Of A City

If a picture is worth a thousand words, this one from the turn of the century is worth an entire chapter. This group of tow-headed schoolboys from the Petite Cote area share the obvious pride of the only member of their gang lucky enough to have boots of his own. Forget the high tops. forget the prized labels, just to have shoes is the ultimate. The faces say it all. There is no more.

Photo Album

Sources

Sources And Other Reading

BOOKS

1. BABY, William Lewis. *Souvenirs of the Past.* Windsor: 1896.

2. BEARDEN, Jim, and Linda Burton. *Shadd: Life and Times of Mary Shadd Cary.* Toronto: NC Press Ltd., 1977.

3. BERTON, Pierre. *The Invasion of Canada 1812 -1813.* Toronto: McClelland and Stewart Ltd., 1980.

4. BLACK STUDIES EDUCATION COMMITTEE. *Black Settlements in Southwestern Ontario.* Windsor: The Black Studies Education Committee of Windsor, 1977.

5. BRODE, Patrick. *Alexander Cameron and The Flowering of the County of Essex, 1853-1893.* Occasional Paper No. 4, Essex County Historical Society, Windsor: 1987.

6. CARLESIMO, Peter. "The Refugee Home Society: Its Origin, Operation and Results, 1851-1876." Masters thesis, University of Windsor, 1973.

7. CHAUVIN, Francis X. "Life and Times of Hiram Walker", Hiram Walker, Walkerville. Undated.

8. CHAUVIN, Francis X. *Men of Achievement, Essex County,* Tecumseh: 1927.

9. COUTTS, Grace M. *100 Women of Windsor and Essex County.* Biographical sketches compiled for the Windsor Local Council of Women, 1967.

10. COWAN, HUGH. "The Detroit River District", *Canadian Achievement In the Province of Ontario.* Algonquin Historical Society of Canada; Vol 1, 1929.

11. DOUGLAS, R. Alan. "A Brief Historical Sketch of Windsor and Area." Speech delivered to the Windsor Chamber of Commerce, February, 1962.

12. DOUGLAS, R. Alan. "The Battle of Windsor," *Ontario History.* Vol. LXI, No. 3, September, 1969. Pages 137 to 152.

13. DOUGLAS, R. Alan. *Mansion to Museum, The François Baby House and Its Times.* Windsor: Essex County Historical Society, Occasional Paper No. 5, 1989.

14. FARMER, Silas. *The History of Detroit and Michigan or The Metropolis Illustrated.* Detroit: Silas Farmer & Co., 1884.

15. FULLER, Robert M. *Windsor Heritage.* Windsor: Robert M. Fuller, 1972.

16. GORDON, Donald. *Eighteen Men, the Prime Ministers of Canada.* Toronto: Doubleday, 1985.

17. GURD, Norman S. *The Story of Tecumseh.* Toronto: William Briggs, 1912.

18. HAVRAN, MARTIN J. "Windsor — Its First Hundred Years," *Ontario History.* Ontario Historical Society X1VI, Number 3, 1954. Page 179.

19. HILL, Daniel G. *The Freedom Seekers; Blacks in Early Canada.* Toronto: The Book Society of Canada, 1981.

20. HOLTON, F. J. and D. H. Bedford and Francis Cleary. "History of the Windsor and Detroit Ferries," *Essex Historical Society Papers and Addresses.* Vol 3, 1921. Page 5.

21. HOSKINS, Ronald G. "Historical Survey of the Town of Walkerville 1858-1922." Masters thesis, University of Windsor, 1964.

22. HOSKINS, Ronald G. "Hiram Walker and the Origins and Development of Walkerville," *Ontario History.* Vol. LXIV, Number 3. September, 1972, Page 122.

23. HOWISON, John. *Sketches of Upper Canada;* London: G & W.B. Whittaker, 1821. Facsimile reprint, Toronto. Coles Publishing Company, 1970.

24. HUTCHISON, Bruce. *The Struggle for the Border.* Toronto: Longmans, Green and Co., 1955.

25. JAMESON, Anna. *Winter Studies and Summer Rambles In Canada.* London: Saunders and Otley, 1838. New Canadian Library edition, Toronto: McClelland & Stewart Inc., 1990.

26. JENSON, Carole. "History of the Negro Community in Essex County, 1850-1860." Masters thesis, University of Windsor.

27. KARR, William John. *Explorers, Soldiers and Statesmen*. New York: J. M. Dent & Sons, 1970.

28. LAJEUNESSE, Rev. Ernest J. (CSB). *The Windsor Border Region*. Toronto: The Champlain Society for the Government of Ontario, 1960.

29. LAJEUNESSE, Rev. Ernest J. (CSB). *Assumption Parish 1767-1967*. Windsor; 1967.

30. LAMB, W. Kaye. *The Hero of Upper Canada*. Toronto: Rous and Mann Press Limited, 1962.

31. LOTZ, Jim. *Prime Ministers of Canada*. London: Bison Books Ltd., 1987.

32. MACDONALD, George F. "How Windsor Got its Name," *Essex County Historical Society Papers and Addresses*, Windsor, Vol 3, 1921. Page 33.

33. McCORMICK, William. *Sketch of the Western District of Upper Canada Being the Southern extremity of that interesting Province*. Edited by R. Alan Douglas. Essex County Historical Association and University of Windsor Press, Occasional Paper No. 1, 1980.

34. MORRISON, Neil F. *Garden Gateway to Canada*. Essex County Historical Association (Society), 1954.

35. NEAL, Frederick. *The Township of Sandwich; Past and Present*. Sandwich, 1909; Reprinted by The Essex County Historical Association (Society) and The Windsor Public Library Board, 1979.

36. ONTARIO MINISTRY OF CITIZENSHIP & CULTURE. *An Enduring Heritage: Black Contributions to Early History*. Toronto: Dundurn Press, 1984.

37. POWER, Michael. *Assumption College, Years of Uncertainty 1855-1870*. Windsor: Assumption University, 1987.

38. RANSOME, W.R. (Bill). *Souvenir Book of Olden Times Around the Detroit River & Essex County*. Amherstburg: Past & Present Shop, undated.

39. RICHARDSON, Maj. John. *Richardson's War of 1812*. Toronto: Historical Publishing Company, 1902.

40. ST. MARY'S ACADEMY MEMOIRS: 1861-1977. Souvenir booklet, Windsor: St.Mary's Academy, 1977.

41. SMITH, W. H. *Smith's Canadian Gazetteer*. Toronto: Rowsell, 1846; Facsimile reprint, Toronto: Coles — The Book People!, 1970.

42. THOMAS, Sister John, (Helen Batte). *Rooted in Hope*. Windsor: Holy Names Society of Jesus and Mary, 1983.

43. UNITED EMPIRE LOYALISTS ASSOCIATION OF CANADA. *Loyal She Remains*. Toronto; 1984.

44. *Walking Tour of Historic Sandwich Town*. Windsor Architectural Conservation Advisory Committee. A self-guided tour, Windsor: (1984) 1986.

45. *Walking Tour Through Old Walkerville*. Windsor Architectural Conservation Advisory Committee. A self-guided tour, Windsor: (1984) 1986.

46. WALLS, Dr. Bryan E. *The Road that Led to Somewhere*. Windsor: Olive Publishing Company Ltd., 1980.

47. WESTGATE, Ven. Archdeacon H. Palmer. *A Goodly Heritage; St. John's Anglican Church 1802-1952*. Windsor; 1952.

48. WINKS, Robin W. *The Blacks in Canada, A history*. Montreal: McGill-Queen's University Press.

NEWSPAPERS

49. WEEKLY RECORD, 1892; Windsor Public Library.

50. VOICE OF THE FUGITIVE, 1851; Leddy Library, University of Windsor.

51. PROVINCIAL FREEMAN, 1853; Leddy Library, University of Windsor.

52. CANADIAN EMIGRANT, 1836; Leddy Library, University of Windsor.

53. MICHIGAN CATHOLIC, September 27, 1888; Hotel Dieu Archives.

54. WINDSOR STAR, Microfilm Archives, Windsor Star Library.